1000 Sopranos Facts

Scott Ambrose

Contents

INTRODUCTION

1000 Sopranos Facts dives deep into the world of mob boss Tony Soprano and his dysfunctional crime family. Packed with information, behind-the-scenes stories, and trivia, this book is a must-have for any fan of the groundbreaking HBO series. Discover the real-life inspirations for the characters, the filming locations, and the memorable moments that made The Sopranos a cultural phenomenon. Grab your cannoli and settle in for a fascinating journey through the world of The Sopranos.

1000 SOPRANOS FACTS

(1) HBO didn't like The Sopranos as the title of the show and suggested it should be called The Family Man. Thankfully, they didn't get their way on this.

(2) The exterior of Tony Soprano's house in the show was depicted by a real estate in North Caldwell, New Jersey. 150 houses were scouted by the production before they chose this one. The house was owned by Victor and Patti Recchia - who co-operated with the production for exterior and backyard shooting. In 2019, it was reported in the media that the house was up for sale for $3.4 million.

(3) The gun logo representing the 'r' in the logo for The Sopranos was designed to make sure no one presumed the show was about singers.

(4) Dan Castleman, an assistant D.A. in New York, was technical consultant on the show. Sopranos creator David Chase said that Castleman estimated that Tony Soprano's net worth would amount to about $6 million. Adjusted for inflation that figure would obviously be higher in today's money but Tony Soprano wasn't outrageously rich by (fictional) criminal standards. Take Gus Fring in Breaking Bad for example. Fring was making millions of dollars a month from his meth empire.

(5) Tony Soprano's obsession with ducks might be inspired by Holden Caulfield in J.D Salinger's The Catcher in the Rye. Holden frequently wonders in the novel where the ducks in Central Park go in the Winter when the lakes are frozen. The ducks are a symbol of how one must adapt to the circumstances which present themselves. Holden must be willing to do the same. He has to accept change as an unavoidable consequence of life. Holden's cab driver tells him that Mother Nature will find a solution to the ducks. This is a

soothing piece of wisdom that could apply to Holden too. The ducks in The Sopranos may represent Tony's fear of his family 'flying the nest' and leaving him alone. The ducks return to Tony's pool before flying away, symbolizing the fleeting nature of happiness and the inevitability of change. This scene is open to interpretation, with some viewers seeing it as a symbol of Tony's eventual demise or departure from his criminal lifestyle.

(6) The first four seasons of The Sopranos were released on VHS. By the time of season five, DVDs had all but replaced VHS tapes so there was no VHS release.

(7) The food you see the characters eating in The Sopranos came from real Italian restaurants. This is why the actors are often really eating and not just pushing the food around.

(8) Tobin Bell played Major Carl Zwingli, the official at the military school Tony is attempting to put his son AJ into in season three. Bell would later become best known for his role as Jigsaw in the Saw horror film franchise.

(9) Vito Antuofermo was in two episodes of The Sopranos as Bobby Zanone. Bobby runs Zanone Bros. Private Carting - a garbage haulage transfer station company front business for the Aprile crew. Vito Antuofermo is a former professional boxer. He was born on April 9, 1953, in Palo del Colle, Italy. Antuofermo is best known for winning the world middleweight boxing championship in 1979 by defeating Hugo Corro. He defended his title once (a controversial draw with Marvin Hagler) before losing it to Alan Minter. Vito Antuofermo also had a small part in The Godfather Part III.

(10) The inspiration for the name of Tony's mother Livia is that a maternal aunt of David Chase had this name. The name was also apt because it evoked Livia Drusilla. Livia Drusilla was the third wife of the Roman emperor Augustus. She was born in 58 BC and married Augustus in 38 BC. Livia was a powerful and influential figure in Roman politics, often acting

as a trusted advisor to her husband. She was also known for her intelligence, cunning, and ambition.

(11) Phil Leotardo, when he learns that Vito is gay/bisexual, refers to Vito as a 'fanook'. This comes from the Italian word 'finocchio' – which means fennel. Finocchio can be used as a derogatory term for a homosexual man in Italian slang. The origin allegedly derives from the middle ages when homosexuals were burned at the stake and fennel seeds were scattered on the site afterwards.

(12) Anthony LaPaglia was allegedly the studio's first choice for the part of Tony Soprano when the show was in development at Fox before moving to HBO. Anthony LaPaglia is an Australian actor best known for his roles in films such as Lantana, Empire Records, and Balibo. He also had a starring role in the TV series Without a Trace, for which he won a Golden Globe Award. LaPaglia has confirmed that he was approached to play Tony Soprano but said that it was for the best that James Gandolfini got the part because no one could have played it better.

(13) Steve Schirripa (who played Bobby) said one of his oddest memories on The Sopranos was eating chicken cacciatore for a scene that involved Bobby, Feech and Tony. Nothing strange about that you might think. The only thing is, the scene was shot at 7 in the morning! Chicken cacciatore is a classic Italian dish that features chicken cooked in a flavorful tomato-based sauce with onions, garlic, bell peppers, and sometimes mushrooms. Not the sort of thing you'd want to be eating first thing in the morning.

(14) The Mafia is also known as La Cosa Nostra. This translates into 'our thing'.

(15) Will Janowitz, who played Meadow's boyfriend Finn DeTrolio, had never actually heard of The Sopranos when he was offered an audition.

(16) Dan Grimaldi, who played Patsy Parisi, is actually a mathematics professor in real life. It seems quite apt then that Patsy is often seen as the accountant for Tony's crew!

(17) The reason why Tony Soprano doesn't want Vito Spatafore killed is that Vito is Tony's biggest earner. Tony is also plainly less bothered by Vito's bisexuality than old school mob figures like Phil Leotardo (who is Vito's cousin-in-law). The conflict over what to do with Vito touches upon a recurring undercurrent theme in the show - the struggles of the mob to adjust to the modern world.

(18) The characters in The Sopranos refer to pasta sauce as 'gravy'. The term 'gravy' used to refer to tomato sauce or marinara sauce on pasta is likely a regional Italian-American colloquialism. In Italian cuisine, gravy generally refers to meat-based sauces, such as ragu or Bolognese. However, Italian immigrants in America may have started using the term gravy to refer to tomato sauce because of similarities between the two sauces in terms of preparation and appearance.

(19) In 2005, a young man named Jason Bautista was arrested in Riverside, California, after murdering his mother. After the murder he removed the head and hands to make identification more difficult. Bautista told the police he got the idea for this dismemberment after watching the episode of The Sopranos where Ralphie Cifaretto is chopped up.

(20) In the episode Pine Barrens, Paulie famously muddles up Czechoslovakians with Chechens. Chechens are an ethnic group native to Chechnya, a region in the North Caucasus in Russia. They have a distinct language and culture, and have a long history of conflict with Russia.

(21) Paulie Gualtieri's nickname 'Walnuts' is never actually explained. There is a theory that he got this name because he robbed a truck and it had nothing but walnuts in it.

(22) Tony's mother Livia Soprano had a final scene in season three - despite the death Nancy Marchand (who obviously played Livia). Digital compositing and a stand-in was used to depict Livia in her final scene. Old lines of dialogue used by Nancy Marchand were deployed in the scene to make it look as if Livia is having a conversation with Tony - or at least responding to him. It is probably fair to say that the special effects in this scene have not aged very well. It is patently obvious that this is fake and isn't really Nancy Marchand. David Chase argued that the scene was necessary because the audience needed one last moment with the choleric Livia to remind ourselves of her character before her death occurred in the show and the stories moved on beyond Tony's relationship with his mother. David Chase has admitted the 'early CGI' in Livia's last appearance could have been better.

(23) In the scene where Tony calls in Christopher to help him cut up Ralphie's body, Michael Imperioli gives a noticeably strange line reading of the word 'didn't' - which was left in because Christopher was high and so it made sense that he's mangling words. Michael Imperioli's 'drug addled' acting in this scene is brilliant.

(24) The episode Pine Barrens was not actually filmed in the Pine Barrens. It was shot at Harriman State Park - which is 30 miles north of New York.

(25) In the opening credits to The Sopranos, Tony begins his car journey in the Lincoln Tunnel. The Lincoln Tunnel is a three-tube tunnel that connects New York City to New Jersey underneath the Hudson River. It was opened in 1937 and is an important transportation link for commuters and travelers between the two states. The tunnel is named after President Abraham Lincoln and is one of the busiest vehicular tunnels in the United States.

(26) Joe Pantoliano based his wig as Ralphie Cifaretto on the film director Christopher Nolan! Pantoliano had recently worked with Nolan on Memento.

(27) James Gandolfini sounds different as Tony in the pilot than he did in the series which followed. He sounds more New Jersey in the series than the pilot.

(28) David Chase said that The Sopranos, when you boiled it right down, was about money and death.

(29) Bobby, amusingly, gets Quasimodo muddled up with Nostradamus. Nostradamus was a French astrologer, physician, and reputed seer who lived in the 16th century. He is best known for his book of prophecies, "Les Propheties," which contains cryptic predictions about future events. Many people believe that Nostradamus accurately predicted several major world events, while others argue that his prophecies are vague and open to interpretation.

(30) There is a fan theory that the onion rings in the last ever scene symbolise the last communion - meaning that Tony, Carmela, and AJ got whacked. Suffice to say, David Chase has never confirmed this alleged subtext.

(31) The highest ranked episode of The Sopranos on IMDB is a tie between Long Term Parking and Pine Barrens. Both have a rating of 9.7.

(32) The singer Lady Gaga (who at the time was obviously still going by her real name Stefani Germanotta) appeared in The Sopranos episode The Telltale Moozadell. Gaga is one of the girls at the swimming pool who laughs. She has made light of her Sopranos appearance and admitted she didn't know much about acting at the time.

(33) The mafia still exists today in the United States but in a diminished form compared to past decades. This is a theme that The Sopranos obviously touches upon. Tony Soprano was born into a tradition which no longer has the power and influence it once did and may even be threatened with extinction. Being a mob boss at the dawn of the 21st century feels like an anachronism.

(34) Steven Van Zandt was best known for his work as a guitarist in Bruce Springsteen's E Street Band. He wasn't an actor when he was cast in The Sopranos as Silvio Dante but David Chase (who clearly must be a Bruce Springsteen fan) had a hunch that Steven would be great in the show.

(35) Steven Van Zandt was considered for the part of Tony Soprano but in the end they obviously decided not to go with an inexperienced actor as the lead.

(36) Silvio Dante is the consigliere to Tony Soprano. The term "consigliere" is an Italian word that has been adopted into English. It refers to a trusted advisor or counselor, especially in a mafia or criminal organization. A consigliere is someone who provides guidance, advice, and wisdom to the leader of the organization.

(37) In 2000, a casting call for The Sopranos in the New Jersey town of Harrison had to be shut down when 13,000 hopefuls turned up.

(38) David Chase said that when the show was in the planning stage they did reach out to a former mafia member to be an advisor but then decided this wasn't a good idea.

(39) The interior scenes set in the Soprano house were shot at Silver Cup Studios. Silvercup Studios is one of the largest film and television production facilities in New York City. The studio is located in Long Island City, Queens. The exception was the pilot - in which some scenes were actually shot inside the North Caldwell, New Jersey home which was used as Tony Soprano's house in the show.

(40) David Chase later confessed that he wasn't exactly sure what he was trying to say with the plot about Christopher meeting Hollywood film stars. He suspects he might have been attempting to draw parallels with between the mafia and Hollywood - which are both full of ambitious sociopaths!

(41) Jamie-Lynn Sigler and Robert Iler, who played Tony Sopranos's kids, are not of Italian descent in real life. This made them quite rare in the cast.

(42) Peter Bogdanovich played Elliot Kupferberg in The Sopranos. Elliot is the therapist of Dr Jennifer Melfi. Peter Bogdanovich was primarily a film director best known for The Last Picture Show and Paper Moon. He was also well known due to his association with Dorothy Stratten. Dorothy Stratten was an actress, model and Playboy playmate. She appeared in Buck Rogers in the 25th Century, Fantasy Island, and the bargain basement but cultish sci-fi film Galaxina. She also got a small part in the Peter Bogdanovich film They All Laughed. Bogdanovich fell in love with Stratten and they began an affair. The only problem was that Stratten was married to a pimp and hustler named Paul Snider.

Stratten wanted to start a new life with Bogdanovich and so arranged to meet Snider (from whom she was estranged) to ask for a divorce. Stratten was advised by Bogdanovich not to go and meet Snider but she did so anyway. Dorothy Stratten met Snider in the home they used to share and it would tragically be the last night of her life. Snider turned up with a shotgun and killed Stratten by shooting her in the face. She was only twenty years-old. Snider then shot himself. Bogdanovich was devastated by Dorothy Stratten's death. Several years later he raised a few eyebrows by marrying Dorothy's younger sister Louise. The marriage lasted until 2001. Two films were made based on this sad case in the wake of Dorothy Stratten's death - Death of a Centerfold: The Dorothy Stratten Story and Star 80 starring Mariel Hemingway.

(43) One of Tony Soprano's most iconic fashion items is the humble bathrobe. Tony is often seen in a big white bathrobe when he's at home.

(44) The newspaper Tony Soprano has delivered is the Star-Ledger. The Star-Ledger is the largest circulation newspaper in

New Jersey.

(45) Edie Falco was 34 years-old when she played Carmela Soprano in the pilot for The Sopranos. Jamie-Lynn Sigler, who played Carmela's daughter Meadow in The Sopranos, is now 42 in real life.

(46) Over the course of The Sopranos, subscriptions to HBO went up by 50%. The Sopranos was a big part of this spike.

(47) David Chase said in an interview that Carmela Soprano had 'done a deal with the Devil' by staying married to Tony - despite being aware of what he really did for a living.

(48) Tony Soprano pretends to be a waste management consultant at Barone Sanitation. In reality this is the company he uses to launder money and he's really a mob boss in New Jersey. Tony's real income comes from typical mafia activities like loan-sharking, extortion, gambling, robberies, and union corruption. As the boss, all of the members of Tony's crew must pay him a slice from their criminal activities.

(49) Jamie-Lynn Sigler released a pop album in 2001 to try and cash in on her Sopranos fame. The album didn't do very well and Jamie-Lynn has since said she didn't especially enjoy her singing interlude. Jamie said her singing on the album was faked too.

(50) When the show was still running, the Italian-American Anti-Defamation League actually arranged a meeting with David Chase to explain their gripes about The Sopranos. It transpired though that none of them had actually watched the show so they were complaining about something they'd never even seen.

(51) Frankie Valli played the vertically challenged Rusty Millio in The Sopranos. Rusty is a capo in the Lupertazzi Family. Frankie Valli was inducted into the Rock and Roll Hall of Fame as a member of the Four Seasons in 1990.

(52) Drea de Matteo said that when her time on The Sopranos came to an end she took home the tiger-print spandex onesie that Adriana had. She was also allowed to take home the outfit that Adriana was wearing when she got whacked.

(53) The year that The Sopranos came out there was a film with an uncannily similar premise. Analyze This is a 1999 film directed by Harold Ramis. The film follows the story of a powerful mob boss named Paul Vitti, played by Robert De Niro, who begins experiencing anxiety attacks and seeks out the help of a therapist, Dr Ben Sobel, played by Billy Crystal. Apparently it was just a coincidence that The Sopranos and Analyze This had a similar premise. Neither was influenced by the other. The big difference is that Analyze This was a comedy whereas The Sopranos is a drama.

(54) In the episode The Telltale Moozadell, Tony refers to Edgar Allan Poe as 'the guy that did all the Vincent Price s***'. Vincent Price appeared in a number of AIP horror films based on Poe's work. Edgar Allan Poe (1809-1849) was an American writer, poet, and literary critic best known for his macabre and Gothic tales. He is known for works like The Raven and The Fall of the House of Usher.

(55) Tony calls Christopher his nephew but in reality Christopher is Tony's cousin by marriage (Christopher is Carmela's cousin).

(56) Jerry Stiller was supposed to play Herman "Hesh" Rabkin on The Sopranos but he withdrew shortly before the pilot and was replaced by Jerry Adler. Jerry Stiller was known for his comic roles in television shows such as Seinfeld and The King of Queens.

(57) Denise Borino-Quinn played Ginny Sacramoni - the wife of Johnny Sack in the show. Denise tagged along to the audition to support a friend but ended up being cast herself. She never acted in anything else either before or after The Sopranos. Sadly, Denise Borino-Quinn died of cancer in 2010

at the age of 46.

(58) Goomah is Italian slang for mistress or girlfriend. It derives from 'comare' - which means second mother.

(59) It is sometimes reported that the late Ray Liotta turned down the part of Tony Soprano. This is not true but Ray Liotta did say he discussed being in the show later on (possibly for the part of Ralphie, which was played by Joe Pantoliano). The reason he turned it down is that he didn't want to do another mafia part after Goodfellas and was also busy filming Hannibal for Ridley Scott. He felt television would be a step down for his career (which shows how much things have changed because Hollywood actors do television and streaming shows all the time now). Ray Liotta did though later appear in The Many Saints of Newark.

(60) A very young Michael B. Jordan made a brief appearance in the Sopranos episode Down Neck.

(61) Tony Soprano was partly inspired by Vincent Palermo. Palermo (who is still alive at the time of writing) was the boss of the New Jersey DeCavalcante crime family and ended up in witness protection. He owned a strip-club called Wiggles - which was the inspiration behind the Bada Bing! strip-club in The Sopranos.

(62) There was a famous incident in 2002 where James Gandolfini vanished from the Sopranos set and then four days later telephoned from a beauty salon in Brooklyn.

(63) The straight to DVD style horror film that Christopher produces is called Cleaver. Christopher uses the film to lace in some of his real life anxieties and experiences. The film is described as Saw meets the Godfather or the Ring meets The Godfather. The plot has a mobster being murdered but then coming back to life to get revenge.

(64) Tony Soprano seems to love Honey Comb cereal. Honey

Comb cereal is a popular breakfast cereal made by Post Consumer Brands. It is known for its unique honeycomb-shaped pieces that are crispy and sweet.

(65) Barbara Giglione is the sister of Tony and Janice. Barbara is not a major character in the show and usually turns up at functions and family emergencies. Nicole Burdette played this character in seasons two and three and then Danielle Di Vecchio took over the role in seasons five and six.

(66) The pilot episode was shot in 1997 - two years before The Sopranos actually went to air.

(67) In the scene where Silvio drives Adriana out into the woods to kill her (Sil is pretending he's driving her to hospital to visit Christopher) there is a moment where Sil's expression changes from sympathetic to cold and unemotional. It's a chilling moment because we see that Sil has decided to end the charade. He doesn't care whether Adrianahas deduced what is really happening because it is already too late for her.

(68) Jim "Johnny Cakes" Witowski, the lover of Vito Spatafore, was played by John Costelloe, Sadly, John Costelloe shot himself in 2008 at the age of 47.

(69) In the prequel film The Many Saints of Newark, Silvio Dante is revealed to be bald and wearing a toupee. This somewhat clashed with The Sopranos - where Silvio is seen to have hair even when he's fighting for his life in hospital. Surely they would have taken his wig off wouldn't they?

(70) Because the last ever episode of The Sopranos abruptly cuts to black at a slightly unexpected moment, some viewers who were watching at the time thought there was something wrong with their television and they'd missed the real ending!

(71) David Chase said that Phil Leotardo is secretly a closeted gay man (and in the mob no less) - which is why Phil is so obsessed with Vito's sexuality and so vocal about getting

revenge.

(72) James Gandolfini came to the attention of The Sopranos casting director after she saw him in the film True Romance. True Romance is a 1993 romantic crime film directed by Tony Scott and written by Quentin Tarantino. It stars Christian Slater and Patricia Arquette as a young couple on the run from the mob.

(73) There was a court case in 2007 in which Robert Baer, a former judge, claimed that he helped create The Sopranos by introducing David Chase to police and prosecutors - thus (so Mr Baer claimed) sowing the seed for the show. Baer also seemed to claim that he helped write the pilot. The claims of Mr Baer were rejected by the court. After the verdict, David Chase described Mr Baer as a "buzzing fly that has finally been swatted."

(74) Joe Pantoliano only found out his character Ralphie was going to be killed during a table read. According to other cast members he jumped up, got on the phone to his agent, and stormed out.

(75) On June the 19th, 2013, James Gandolfini was in Rome enjoying a holiday. He was with his wife and young son Michael and due to accept an award in Italy as part of the trip. chance. At around nine in the evening, Michael found James Gandolfini passed out unconscious in the bathroom of their hotel room. Michael called for help and an ambulance was summoned after hotel staff failed in their efforts to revive the actor. James Gandolfini was taken to the Policlinico Umberto I hospital but died shortly after arriving. He was 51 years-old. James Gandolfini's cause of death was a massive heart-attack.

The actor's family and those that had worked with him were devastated by his death. It was a great loss to the acting world too because he still had many great roles ahead of him - which would now sadly never come to pass. A funeral service was held at the Cathedral Church of St. John the Divine in New

York. It was attended by Sopranos cast members and many celebrities.

(76) The Twin Towers in New York were destroyed in the 9/11 attack while The Sopranos was in production. The towers featured in the title sequence when the show began but were removed from the titles after the terrorist attack.

(77) The mafia originated in Sicily, Italy.

(78) Tony Soprano is a big fan of Gary Cooper. Gary Cooper was an American actor known for his roles in classic western films such as High Noon and The Westerner. He had a distinguished career spanning over four decades and won two Academy Awards for Best Actor. Cooper was also known for his quiet, understated acting style and his masculine, stoic on-screen presence.

(79) Michael Rispoli was strongly considered for the part of Tony Soprano but obviously lost out in the end. He did though take the part of Giacomo "Jackie" Aprile Sr.

(80) It was the director Tim Van Patten who came up with the idea of Pine Barrens. He pitched an idea where two of Tony's mobsters take someone out into the forest to shoot them but lose their prisoner and then lose their bearings and get lost. He said it was actually a dream which gave him the idea.

(81) Phil Leotardo refers to Tony's crew as 'farmers' in the show. Farmers is a term that the New York mafia use to refer to the New Jersey mafia.

(82) The name Meadow was inspired by the name tag of a waitress who served David Chase in a coffee shop. It struck David as a very interesting and unusual name.

(83) Tony Soprano is very partial to cannoli. Cannoli are a classic Italian pastry typically made by deep frying tubes of dough filled with a sweet, creamy filling. The filling is often

made with ricotta cheese, sugar, and sometimes chocolate chips or candied fruit. The cannoli are then typically dusted with powdered sugar and sometimes sprinkled with pistachios or chocolate shavings.

(84) Vera Farmiga, who played Livia in The Many Saints of Newark, unsuccessfully auditioned to play Valentina La Paz (the mistress of Ralphie Cifaretto) in The Sopranos. It was Leslie Bega who bagged this part in the end.

(85) Vincent Pastore, who played Salvatore 'Big Pussy' Bonpensiero, said in a 2020 interview that he was annoyed his character got killed off fairly early in the show and he stopped watching it after he left. Pastore said the cast were on good wages so losing that money was tough to take - plus of course he was losing the exposure of being in such a big show.

(86) Adriana's arc in the show was loosely inspired by Theresa Ferrara. Ferrara was the mistress of Lucchese crime family associate Thomas DeVito. When she was busted for drugs she became an FBI informant. She was murdered by the mafia - her dismembered body found floating in a river.

(87) Tony's fish themed dream in Funhouse was shot on the boardwalk at Asbury Park. Asbury Park is a popular beach town located on the Jersey Shore in New Jersey.

(88) Vito Spatafore is revealed to be secretly gay/bisexual in The Sopranos. This ultimately leads to his death because the mafia is not exactly famous for its tolerance of homosexuality. Joe Gannascoli, who played Vito, said it was him who had the idea of Vito being gay. He got the idea after reading a book about Vito Arena. Arena was a gay mobster in the Gambino crime family but had to keep his sexuality secret. Another inspiration for the Vito storyline was John "Johnny Boy" D'Amato. D'Amato was the former acting boss of the DeCavalcante crime family in New Jersey from 1990 to 1992. He was murdered by mafia members in 1992 after rumors that he was bisexual came to light in the mob.

(89) The title song in The Sopranos is Woke Up This Morning by Alabama 3. Alabama 3 are a British group who were founded after some of the original members met at an acid house party in London.

(90) David Proval, who played Richie Aprile, said he was absolutely furious when he was told that Richie was going to be killed and he was off the show.

(91) Maureen Van Zandt, who play Sil's wife Gabriella Dante, is Steven Van Zandt's wife in real life.

(92) Tony Sirico was connected to the Columbo crime family in his younger years. He never became a 'made man' though and said in interviews that he never killed anyone. Paulie mentions the 'Columbos going at it in the 70s' in The Sopranos.

(93) In the pilot Tony and his crew hang around outside Centanni's Meat Market - which is a real store in Elizabeth, New Jersey. This was replaced by the fictional Satriale's in the actual show. Satriale's was depicted by a vacant building (which was obviously dressed to look like a real meat store) at 101 Kearny Ave in Kearny, New Jersey. This building was torn down in 2007. Satriale's was recreated for The Many Saints of Newark in another part of New Jersey.

(94) Among the hoodies and t-shirts that AJ Soprano wears in the show are ones for Slipknot, Pantera and Marilyn Manson.

(95) Edie Falco had the flu when they shot the Paris scenes in Cold Stones and had almost lost her voice. She re-recorded much of Carmela's dialogue back in the United States.

(96) The Pine Barrens, also known as the Pinelands, is a heavily forested area in the coastal plain of New Jersey. The Pine Barrens cover over 1 million acres and are home to a variety of wildlife. The area has been preserved and protected by the New Jersey Pinelands Commission.

(97) One of the inspirations for The Sopranos was the DeCavalcante crime family in New Jersey. The DeCavalcante crime family is known for its close ties to the Five Families of New York City, particularly the Lucchese crime family. The family has undergone various leadership changes and internal conflicts over the years, but it has remained a presence in the New Jersey underworld. The DeCavalcante crime family has been the target of numerous law enforcement investigations and prosecutions, leading to the arrest and conviction of many of its members.

(98) In an interview, James Gandolfini said that the first season episode College was one of his favorites. In this episode we see both sides of Tony Soprano. His role as a father when he takes Meadow to visit colleges she is thinking of attending and his role as a vengeful mob boss when he spots a 'rat' who entered witness protection after testifying.

(99) The Sopranos is credited with ushering in what is sometimes known as the first golden age of television. Alongside other acclaimed shows of that era (like Six Feet Under and The Wire) it created a sense of 'prestige television' where the best shows on the small screen were now on a par with cinema.

(100) The Genovese family's Boiardo crew were a particular influence on David Chase when he wrote The Sopranos. This real life crew operated in Newark.

(101) When the sad news of James Gandolfini's passing was announced, fans of The Sopranos left candles and flowers at the North Caldwell, New Jersey home which was used as Tony Soprano's house in the show.

(102) The writers on the show said they especially loved writing for Uncle Junior because Uncle Junior is famously blunt and foul-mouthed. Uncle Junior was the character who made the writers laugh the most.

(103) David Chase has said there are no hidden meanings in the way The Sopranos ends and that people have tended to overthink that last scene.

(104) Ziti is a type of pasta that is similar to penne, but with a larger and longer shape. It is often used in baked pasta dishes like ziti al forno, where it is layered with sauce and cheese and then baked until bubbly and golden brown. AJ likes ziti.

(105) When the last ever episode of The Sopranos went out, David Chase slipped away to France so he could avoid all the American reviews and interview requests!

(106) The episode of The Sopranos with the biggest viewing figures for HBO was the fourth season opener - which drew 13.4 million viewers.

(107) Vera Farmiga looks uncannily like Carmela Soprano as Livia in The Many Saints of Newark. This was probably not a coincidence.

(108) Robert Iler, who played Tony Soprano's son AJ, retired from acting in his thirties to be a part-time poker player. He only had a few credits after The Sopranos.

(109) David Chase said that the use of dreams in The Sopranos was inspired by his love of David Lynch.

(110) In the early plans for the show, Tony Soprano was going to be called Tommy Soprano.

(111) Christopher Moltisanti drives a Lexus LS400 in season one.

(112) Paulie Gualtieri always drives a Cadillac. He has a number of different models in the show.

(113) The F-word was used 3,508 times in The Sopranos.

(114) Some crime commentators have suggested that The Sopranos is slightly unrealistic in the way that Tony's New Jersey operation seems to be an equal of the New York mob and even have the ability to take them on.

(115) Fox developed The Sopranos for a little bit before it went to HBO. David Chase said he felt this was a lucky break because HBO had more faith and trust in the show than the other networks.

(116) John Ventimiglia read for a number of roles in The Sopranos, including Paulie Walnuts, before being given the role of the chef Artie Bucco. Ventimiglia said he was rather dismayed to be given this part but he enjoyed it much more than he thought.

(117) Ralph Cifaretto is a big fan of the film Gladiator. Gladiator is a historical drama directed by Ridley Scott and released in 2000. The story follows a Roman general named Maximus Decimus Meridius, played by Russell Crowe, who is betrayed and seeks revenge against the corrupt emperor.

(118) In a 2024 article, Esquire ranked The Sopranos as the second greatest HBO show of all time. The Wire was in first place.

(119) David Chase told the media in 2002 that the fifth season of The Sopranos would be his last - which obviously didn't turn out to be the case. David said that as HBO owned The Sopranos they could carry it on without him if they decided to. After these comments a number of cast members went on record to say they definitely wouldn't appear in The Sopranos anymore if David Chase wasn't involved.

(120) Bobby Baccalieri Sr was played by Burt Young - who was best known for his role as Paulie in the Rocky series.

(121) In the late 1990s, the FBI recorded two members of the The DeCavalcante crime family discussing The Sopranos and

pondering whether the show was supposed to be based on them.

(122) One reason why some believe Tony got 'whacked' in the last ever scene is that Tony's favorite scene in The Godfather was when Michael Corleone shoots Sollozzo and Captain McCluskey in a restaurant.

(123) James Gandolfini said in an interview that Uncle Junior was his favorite character in the show.

(124) James Gandolfini was 37 years-old when the pilot for The Sopranos first aired. Robert Iler, who played Tony Soprano's son AJ, is actually older than that in real life now.

(125) The video game that Tony and AJ play in Meadowlands is Mario Kart 64.

(126) The episode Commendatori did Italian location shooting in Naples, Monte di Procida, and Bacoli.

(127) Tony's first mistress - or goomah - in the show is the young Russian woman Irina Peltsin. Irina was played by the Ukrainian actress Oksana Lada in the series. In the pilot this character was played by Siberia Federico (who is Italian in real life). Oksana Lada appeared in a number of television shows after The Sopranos but Siberia Federico appears to have given up acting because her last IMBD credit was in 1997.

(128) David Chase originally pitched The Sopranos a movie. Happily though his idea morphed into a long form television show.

(129) The FBI Agent Deborah Ciccerone was originally played by Fairuza Balk. However, when Balk became unavailable she was replaced by Lola Glaudini and Fairuza Balk's scenes were reshot with Glaudini. In the DVD release this character is only played by Lola Glaudini but in the original television transmissions the Fairuza Balk scenes were shown.

(130) Joe Pantoliano, who played Ralphie Cifaretto, said he has never watched The Sopranos. Joe said his character was very dark and so he wouldn't especially want to revisit that.

(131) Christopher Moltisanti drives a Mercedes-Benz CLK in season two.

(132) Fox, after developing the show for a while, turned down The Sopranos. They didn't like the therapy sessions part of the show - which they presumably feared might be a bit dull or unrelatable for viewers.

(133) It would be fair to say the prequel film The Many Saints of Newark got a mixed reception. It has a rating of 6.3 on IMDB.

(134) The lowest rated episode of The Sopranos on IMDB is Christopher with 7.8 out of 10. 7.8 is a pretty good rating for most other shows.

(135) In the title sequence, Tony drives past a little building with Pizza Land written on it. This is a real pizzeria at 260 Belleville Turnpike in North Arlington, New Jersey. The pizzeria was founded in 1965 by Pietro DiPiazza. It briefly closed in 2010 but then opened again after gaining new owners.

(136) Paulie 'Walnuts' Gualtieri's name was inspired by Frank Gualtieri - who was a member of the DeCavalcante crime family.

(137) David Chase said the house they used for Tony Soprano's house had specific requirements in that it had to have a swimming pool and a slightly rustic feel. The former was for the ducks and the latter because a mob boss like Tony Soprano is probably going to want a bit of privacy and peace when he goes home.

(138) James Gandolfini gained a fair bit of weight during the

show. It is evident that Tony Soprano is bigger in later seasons.

(139) Ray Liotta said he had never seen a single episode of The Sopranos when he was cast in The Many Saints of Newark.

(140) The Satin Dolls strip club off Route 17 in Lodi, New Jersey, was used to double for the Bada Bing! strip club.

(141) The last ever scene in The Sopranos was shot at Holsten's, an ice cream parlor and chocolate shop in Bloomfield, New Jersey.

(142) Robert Iler, who played Tony Soprano's son AJ, said one of the reasons he didn't do much acting afterwards is that he was 'spoiled' by the fact his first job was The Sopranos. Anything else after that seemed like a step down.

(143) When his bisexuality is revealed, Vito Spatafore hides out in New Hampshire. This is the state where Walter White went into hiding near the end of Breaking Bad.

(144) According to media reports at the time, James Gandolfini threatened to leave The Sopranos before season five because he was unhappy at his salary. HBO threatened to sue Gandolfini but in the end it was all sorted out. James Gandolfini got a big pay hike in season five. HBO were obviously ready to do anything they could to keep him because without Tony Soprano there was no show.

(145) In the mafia you can only become a 'made man' if you are of Italian descent.

(146) Artie's new restaurant is called Nuovo Vesuvio. The original Vesuvio burned down so the volcano themed name is no coincidence by the writers. Punta Dura Restaurant, 4115 34th Ave, Long Island City, NY, was used for exteriors of Nuovo Vesuvio. The interiors were shot in a studio.

(147) When they shot the pilot, neither David Chase nor James Gandolfini had much expectation or optimism about the show becoming a series.

(149) In the classic scene where Finn tells Tony's crew about Vito being gay, notice how Patsy laughs at Christopher's joke near the end. Christopher and Patsy had previously been at loggerheads. The laughter of Michael Imperioli and Dan Grimaldi feels very genuine so you get the impression they were laughing for real doing this scene.

(150) Michael Imperioli and Steve Schirripa started a Talking Sopranos podcast in 2020. They were inspired to do so because so many people were watching The Sopranos during the lockdowns. Because the show began in the late 1990s there are young people discovering the show all the time.

(151) Michael Imperioli had never actually watched The Sopranos since it ended until he started doing the podcasts during the pandemic.

(152) Silvio Dante was always presumed to be a school friend of Tony Soprano - and this is the backstory that Steven Van Zandt always cited. The Many Saints of Newark contradicts this though as Silvio is depicted as being a decade or so older than Tony in the prequel.

(153) The Sopranos frequently uses dreams and hallucinations to explore the characters' inner thoughts and fears. These symbolic sequences often reveal hidden motivations and emotions, providing insight into the characters' complex psyches.

(154) An incredible 27 actors appeared in both Goodfellas and The Sopranos.

(155) Rolling Stone ranked The Sopranos as the greatest television show ever made in 2022.

(156) Steven Van Zandt appeared in 78 episodes as Silvio.

(157) A made man in the mafia is a title is typically bestowed upon individuals who have proven their loyalty and commitment to the organization. To become a made man, one must go through a secretive initiation ceremony, usually involving swearing allegiance to the mafia family. Made men have certain benefits within the organization, such as protection and access to more resources.

(158) James Gandolfini's real speaking voice was surprisingly different to how Tony Soprano speaks - which only adds more credit to his amazing performance.

(159) After the episode Pine Barrens, a lot of fans presumed that the Russian who escaped from Christopher and Paulie was setting up a later storyline. However, the missing Russian was never actually mentioned again. David Chase said there was never any intention to follow up on this story and was somewhat bemused that he kept getting asked about it.

(160) David Proval, who played Richie Aprile, was seriously considered for the part of Tony Soprano.

(161) David Chase was supposed to direct The Many Saints of Newark but he withdrew because of a heart attack. Alan Taylor (who had directed on The Sopranos) took over as director.

(162) Tony Soprano loves Chinese food. He was highly irritated when the leftover chicken lo mein was gone from the fridge in the strip club.

(163) The Sopranos was the first cable TV show to earn an Emmy nomination for Outstanding Drama Series in its first year eligible.

(164) The digital effects for the 'CG Livia' in Proshai Livushka apparently cost $250,000 - which is amazing given how bad it looks.

(165) David Chase said he had Tony deduce Salvatore 'Big Pussy' Bonpensiero was a rat through a dream because he thought it would be less interesting to do it in a conventional way.

(166) Drea de Matteo had to spend four hours in make-up to turn into Adriana.

(167) The character Carmela Soprano featured in all but one episode of the Sopranos.

(168) In the overall series, Carmela has the most lines after Tony Soprano. Christopher Moltisanti is third and Paulie Gualtieri is fourth.

(169) Eddie Falco said she often had no idea what the actual plots of Sopranos episodes were because she shot most of her scenes Carmela in a kitchen set!

(170) Jamie-Lynn Sigler she loved shooting big dinner and restaurant scenes the most on The Sopranos because she got to interact with more cast members than usual.

(171) David Chase said that one of his slight regrets is killing off Salvatore 'Big Pussy' Bonpensiero so soon because they loved working with Vincent Pastore. However, he felt that 'rat' storyline was too good not to do.

(172) The surname Melfi was inspired by the paternal grandmother of David Chase.

(173) Carmela was the name of a woman that a cousin of David Chase was married. This obviously inspired Carmela Soprano's name.

(174) David Chase said he did a lot of revisions on his Sopranos scripts and some scripts went through a dozen or more versions.

(175) Tony Soprano mentions Henry Hill in the pilot. Henry Hill was an American mobster and associate of the Lucchese crime family who became an FBI informant. After entering the Witness Protection Program, Hill lived under an assumed name and eventually settled in the Seattle area. His life story was later turned into the book Wiseguy by journalist Nicholas Pileggi, which was adapted into Goodfellas by Martin Scorsese.

(176) In the episode The Second Coming, Dr Elliot Kupferberg says his father was a big Untouchables fan. The Untouchables is a crime drama series that aired from 1959 to 1963. Created by Desi Arnaz, the show is based on the memoir of the same name by Eliot Ness and Oscar Fraley, which chronicles the efforts of the Prohibition-era "Untouchables" unit led by Ness to bring down the notorious gangster Al Capone. David Chase said he used to watch this show with his own father.

(177) In the episode From Where to Eternity, AJ is playing on a Game Boy Color. The game he is playing is Pokémon Pinball.

(178) The Sopranos ran for six seasons from 1999 to 2007.

(179) Apparently, the reason why Tony Soprano stabs at his food a lot when he's eating is that James Gandolfini wanted to avoid having to eat too much during a take. It's a common actor trick during a food scene to push their food around rather than actually eat much of it.

(180) Vince Gilligan, the creator of Breaking Bad, said that Walter White was influenced a lot by Tony Soprano. They are different in the sense that Tony was born into crime whereas Walter MOVES into crime but there are certainly similarities in that both face the complications of juggling a secret criminal life with a 'normal' public and private life.

(181) Drew University in Madison, New Jersey was used for the college exteriors in the episode College.

(182) Johnny Sack makes his first appearance in Pax Soprana.

(183) Robert Iler didn't think he would get the part of AJ Soprano Jr because all the other kids at the audition were Italian.

(184) The television show that Janice is watching in Mergers and Acquisitions is Robot Wars. Robot Wars is a British television series that showcases battles between remote-controlled robots. The show first aired in 1998. Contestants build their own robots and compete in various challenges, such as destroying opponents or completing obstacle courses.

(185) Federico Castelluccio, who played Furio Giunta in The Sopranos, was born in Naples. His family moved to New Jersey when he was three years-old.

(186) Tony Soprano is partial to a Bialy. A Bialy is a type of bread that originated in Poland. It is similar to a bagel, but has a round shape and a depression in the center instead of a hole. Bialys are typically filled with onions and poppy seeds and are often enjoyed as a breakfast or snack food.

(187) Joe Gannascoli, who later played Vito Spatafore, actually appeared in season one as a pastry shop customer.

(188) It is probably fair to say that John Magaro's portrayal of Silvio Dante in The Many Saints of Newark was not universally loved by Sopranos fans. The same can be said of the film.

(189) The Sopranos: Road to Respect is a 2006 video game based on the series. The game follows the story of a new character, Joey LaRocca, who is a young mobster looking to make a name for himself in the world of organized crime. As Joey, players will navigate the criminal underworld of New Jersey, interacting with familiar characters from the show such as Tony Soprano, Paulie Walnuts, and Silvio Dante. Players must complete various missions and tasks, such as collecting debts, carrying out hits, and expanding their criminal empire. The game features a mix of third-person action and strategy elements, allowing players to engage in

both hand-to-hand combat and gunfights. As players progress through the game, they will unlock new abilities and upgrades to help them succeed in their criminal endeavors. Road to Respect was published by THQ for the PlayStation 2. The reviews for this game were pretty dire so it is probably for curious Sopranos fans only.

(190) The Sopranos, as an overall series, has a rating of 9.2 on IMDB. The only long form drama shows (excluding miniseries) with a higher rating are Breaking Bad and The Wire.

(191) James Gandolfini was very private and publicity shy for such a big star. He hated talking about himself and doing interviews.

(192) In the prequel film The Many Saints of Newark, the young Tony Soprano dreams of being a football player.

(193) In the episode A Hit Is a Hit, Tony Soprano, in response to a question, says that he once met John Gotti. John Gotti, also known as "The Teflon Don" and "The Dapper Don," was an infamous mobster and boss of the Gambino crime family in New York City. He gained notoriety for his charismatic personality, flashy style, and ruthless tactics in leading the mafia. Gotti was ultimately convicted of multiple crimes, including murder, racketeering, and extortion, and was sentenced to life in prison, where he died in 2002.

(194) Voters on the website Ranker have The Sopranos as the second greatest television drama series ever made. The top spot went to Breaking Bad.

(195) The capo, also known as a captain or captain regime, is in charge of a crew or unit within the mafia organization. They are responsible for overseeing the activities of their crew, collecting money from illegal activities, and reporting to the boss.

(196) Soldiers, also known as made men or wise guys, are lower-ranking members of the mob who carry out the day-to-day criminal activities of the mafia. They are responsible for carrying out orders from their capo and contributing to the profits of the organization.

(197) Tony Soprano often wears retro bowling shirts and polo shirts.

(198) Steve Schirripa (Bobby Baccalieri Jr) said that when he watched The Sopranos for the first time in years for his podcast he was surprised by how funny the show often was.

(199) Robert Iler, who played Tony Soprano's son AJ, said he made (the usually stonefaced) David Chase laugh in his audition when he had to swear. He believes this is what got him the part.

(200) Uncle Junior's name is Corrado Soprano. Corrado was apparently a name that Tony Sirico went by in his younger days.

(201) Johnny Sack, played by Vincent Curatola, was the underboss of Carmine Lupertazzi (of the Brooklyn-based Lupertazzi crime family). The underboss is basically the second in command. Johnny eventually becomes the boss but things obviously don't pan out very well for him in the end.

(202) Tony Soprano has aliases and fake IDs for travel. We see him check into a hotel as Mr Spears.

(203) The mafia flourished in the United States during the Prohibition era, when it became involved in bootlegging and other illegal activities.

(204) David Chase said the only actor who ever asked for a line of dialogue in the show to be changed was Tony Sirico. Tony's complaint was a line where Paulie is called a 'bully'. David Chase said he was happy to take this line out.

(205) The film that Carmela and Father Phil watch in the episode College is The Remains of the Day. The Remains of the Day is a 1993 British-American drama film directed by James Ivory and based on the novel of the same name by Kazuo Ishiguro. The film stars Anthony Hopkins as Stevens, a butler who served at Darlington Hall, a stately home in England, during the early 20th century.

(206) Joe Pantoliano is plainly wearing a wig as Ralphie Cifaretto. This actually became part of the character because it is revealed, after his death, that Ralphie wore a rug.

(207) In 2021, Michael Gandolfini followed in his father's footsteps and played a young version of Tony Soprano in the prequel film The Many Saints of Newark.

(208) Steve Schirripa ran some casinos in Las Vegas before he joined The Sopranos as Bobby.

(209) Christopher Moltisanti drives a Range Rover 4.6 HSE in season three and part of season four.

(210) Tony Sirico had a rather obstreperous youth with many criminal charges. He ended up in prison but a visit by an acting troupe inspired him to take up acting and he managed to have a very long and successful career. Though obviously a bit typecast in mafia roles he did everything from comedy to drama to animation. He was also in six Woody Allen films.

(211) You can tell The Sopranos is a period piece now purely from Christopher's love of Blockbuster Video. Blockbuster Video was a popular chain of video rental stores that was founded in 1985. At its peak, Blockbuster had thousands of locations worldwide and was a dominant force in the home entertainment industry. Customers could rent movies, video games, and other forms of media for a certain period of time before returning them to the store. However, with the rise of online streaming services such as Netflix and the decline of physical media, Blockbuster faced increasing competition and

struggled to adapt to the changing landscape of the industry. The company filed for bankruptcy in 2010. Back in the late 1990s, when The Sopranos started, people still rented VHS tapes from video stores. DVDs had yet to completely take over the market.

(212) Tony Sirico and Frank Vincent both auditioned to play Uncle Junior in The Sopranos. They lost out to Dominic Chianese but it turned out fine in the end as they both got other roles in the show.

(213) Michael Imperioli couldn't actually drive in real life when he was cast in The Sopranos. He was ordered to pass his test and get a license because Christopher obviously had to drive in the show.

(214) Lorraine Bracco was wary of being in The Sopranos because she didn't want to be typecast as the mafia wife/girlfriend - which was the sort of role she got offered all the time after Goodfellas. She was happy to take the part of Dr Jennifer Melfi though because it was a different sort of character. David Chase said it was him who suggested she play Dr Melfi (rather than Carmela) because he thought it might be too obvious and on the nose to have Lorraine play another mafia wife after Goodfellas.

(215) The character Dr Melfi was inspired by real therapy sessions that David Chase had in his life.

(216) David Chase selected all the songs used in the show.

(217) The last episode of The Sopranos was transmitted on June the 10th, 2007.

(218) The episode Pine Barrens deliberately riffs a bit on The Blair Witch Project (which was a fairly recent film at the time) with Christopher and Paulie getting lost in the woods. The Blair Witch Project is a low-budget 1999 horror film directed by Daniel Myrick and Eduardo Sanchez. The film had a clever

and innovative internet marketing campaign and became a box-office smash through good word of mouth despite its minuscule budget. The premise is simple and not entirely original. Three students - Heather Donahue, Joshua Leonard, and Michael C Williams - go hiking into the woods of Burkittsville, Maryland in 1994 to investigate and make a documentary film about a local legend known as the Blair Witch. They are never heard from again but the film they shot with their video equipment is recovered. This shaky footage reveals what happened to them in the Black Hills of Burkittsville.

(219) Tony Sirico always insisted on doing his own hair as Paulie Walnuts. He didn't like the hairdressing department taking over.

(220) Matthew Weiner was a writer on The Sopranos (penning 14 later season episodes) before going on to create the famous AMC show Mad Men.

(221) Vito Spatafore makes his first appearance in The Happy Wanderer.

(222) Tony and Johnny Sack sometimes meet by the Brooklyn Bridge. The Brooklyn Bridge is a historic suspension bridge that crosses the East River in New York City, connecting the boroughs of Manhattan and Brooklyn.

(223) David Chase and star Steven Van Zandt both said that James Gandolfini tried to quit The Sopranos several times because he was so exhausted. James found the combination of juggling The Sopranos with doing movies very tiring and he also found the intensity of playing Tony Soprano very draining.

(224) Jennifer Esposito, who is best known for her role in Blue Bloods, said she twice turned down a chance to audition for a role in The Sopranos. Esposito, who is from New York, said she didn't like the way the show was going to represent Italian

culture and also, having grown up in a place where organized crime was rife, she didn't much care for being in a show about that. Jennifer Esposito has said though that since The Sopranos turned out to be so great that she was probably a bit rash to turn down the chance to be in it.

(225) David Chase said if his Sopranos pilot hadn't gone to series he would have tried to expand it and release it as a movie.

(226) Jamie-Lynn Sigler and Robert Iler reprised their Sopranos roles for a Superbowl commercial in 2022.

(227) Tony Sirico appeared in 74 episodes as Paulie.

(228) Anthony LaPaglia's brother Jonathan LaPaglia appeared in The Sopranos playing himself and 'Michael the Cleaver' from Christopher's horror film.

(229) David Chase originally planned to have Tony Soprano murdered at the end of the show. He was going to have the character die offscreen. In the end they went for the ambiguous (and slightly divisive) ending where the screen suddenly cuts to black as Tony eats out with his family.

(230) James Gandolfini was born in New Jersey in 1961.

(231) Rob Spragg, the songwriter who wrote the show's theme song Woke Up This Morning, said in an interview that he had never actually watched The Sopranos.

(232) James Gandolfini got into acting quite late after taking acting classes at 25.

(233) Michael Imperioli said that, when The Sopranos was still running, people were sometimes disappointed when they met him because he was obviously nothing like Christopher Moltisanti in real life!

(234) Steven Van Zandt said he partly based Sil's relationship with Tony on his own relationship with Bruce Springsteen in the E Street Band. What he meant by this is that he had experience of supporting a friend and 'leader'.

(235) David Chase originally planned to have a plot thread where Tony Soprano (arrested over the airline tickets) has his mother testify against him. In the end though he decided not to do this storyline.

(236) Bobby Baccalieri Jr ranks 13th when it comes to characters in the show with the most lines.

(237) Steven Van Zandt said he was a fan of mafia/crime films and books and grew up in an area where 'wiseguys' were active. As such, despite his acting inexperience, he felt that with The Sopranos he at least was going into something that wasn't completely alien to him.

(238) Michael Imperioli appeared in 80 episodes as Christopher.

(239) David Chase had been in the television industry for a long time before The Sopranos. Among the shows he wrote for are The Rockford Files and Kolchak: The Night Stalker.

(240) Dr Jennifer Melfi ranks fifth when it comes to most lines in the show overall.

(241) Some of the real life old time mafia 'soldiers' now have podcasts and YouTube channels.

(242) James Gandolfini's parents were Italian immigrants so Italy was a very special country to the actor and somewhere he loved to visit when he got the chance.

(243) Jamie-Lynn Sigler said she had to stay out of the sun to get the part of Meadow because she previously looked too tanned to be a New Jersey girl.

(244) Years afterwards, Michael Imperioli was outspoken in the media about a year in which the legal show The Practice won a load of Emmys while The Sopranos was ignored. The idea that The Practice was better than The Sopranos was a preposterous notion to Michael (and many other people too you'd imagine).

(245) Steve Schirripa launched his own pasta sauce in 2015. The product was called Uncle Steve's Sauce. It used Italian tomatoes and is sugar free, gluten free and organic.

(246) Janice Soprano went by the name Parvati Wasatch in her bohemian days.

(247) Cathy Moriarty read for the part of Carmela Soprano. She actually did a 'chemistry audition' with James Gandolfini. Cathy Moriarty is best known for her role as Vicki La Motta in Raging Bull.

(248) The advantage The Sopranos had on HBO is that it could be shown without commercial breaks and without restrictions when it came to violence, language, and sexual content. These factors were important because it would be very difficult to make a show about the mob where no one cussed and there was no violence.

(249) The first episode proper of The Sopranos went out on January 10th, 1999.

(250) The surname Moltisanti is Italian for 'many saints.'

(251) Early in the history of The Sopranos, David Chase seemed to indicate it wouldn't go beyond four seasons. He obviously changed his mind about this in the end.

(252) John Ventimiglia, who played the chef Artie, said he is a pretty good cook in real life too. He said he grew up helping his Italian mother in the kitchen.

(253) David Chase said that the reason we don't see Adriana get shot by Silvio in the woods (it happens offscreen) was more out of respect for the character than trying to be ambiguous.

(254) David Chase said that some of the 'whackings' in The Sopranos were based on newspaper and true accounts of real life mob killings.

(255) Janice has a son named Harpo that she lost custody of. Harpo was not named after the Marx Brother but rather the song Harpo's Blues by Phoebe Snow. Harpo changed his name to Hal in the end anyway.

(256) The books on the shelves in Tony Soprano's house never change during the show. One of the books is The Sicilian by Mario Puzzo - which is set in the Godfather universe.

(257) Tony's son AJ owns a Nintendo 64, Dreamcast, and Xbox 360 through the series.

(258) North Caldwell, New Jersey, where Tony Soprano lives, is regarded to be a very well heeled area. You'd need a large income to live there in Tony's house.

(259) There was an elevated train line close to the studio where The Sopranos was filmed. You can sometimes hear the screech of a train in the background.

(260) In the first episode of season two, the film that Christopher is watching is Key Largo. Key Largo is a 1948 film directed by John Huston and starring Humphrey Bogart, Lauren Bacall, Edward G. Robinson, and Claire Trevor. The film is based on the 1939 play of the same name by Maxwell Anderson. The story follows World War II veteran Frank McCloud (Bogart) who arrives at a hotel in Key Largo, Florida to visit the family of his deceased war buddy. However, the hotel is taken over by a gangster named Johnny Rocco (Robinson) and his crew who are hiding out from the law. As a fierce hurricane approaches the island, tensions rise between

the gangster and the hotel guests, leading to a violent confrontation.

(261) Michael Imperioli wrote four episodes of The Sopranos and also contributed a teleplay.

(262) Drea De Matteo said that when her time on the show as Adriana came to an end the production sent her a pinball machine as a gift.

(263) The episode title Where's Johnny? is an obvious nod to Kubrick's The Shining.

(264) Tony Soprano's basement is oddly cramped compared to the rest of his house. This is because the basement was a studio set and they obviously didn't have room to make it too large.

(265) Season five of The Sopranos was the season with the most deaths. There were 18 deaths in this season.

(266) Drea De Matteo said she actually ended up in The Sopranos as Adriana much longer than originally planned. As such, she wasn't that annoyed when Adriana got killed off because she had a good innings in the show.

(267) David Chase said a big difference between The Sopranos and the real mafia is that in The Sopranos there is more murder and violence than the real life mob.

(268) The season three episode Toodle-F***ing-Oo was directed by Lee Tamahori. A few years later Tamahori directed the next James Bond film - Die Another Day.

(269) Two different versions of Adriana's last scene were shot to try and avoid spoilers leaking. An alternative version where she escaped was done as a sort of fake decoy scene.

(270) John Ventimiglia said he based his character Artie on

Leopoldo Trieste as Signor Roberto in The Godfather Part II.

(271) The juxtaposition of Tony Soprano's suburban family life with his criminal activities reflects larger themes of the American Dream and the dark underbelly of the seemingly idyllic suburban lifestyle.

(272) The precise address of the house used for exterior shots of Tony's house is 14 Aspen Drive in North Caldwell. The address of Tony's house in the show is 633 Stag Trail Road.

(273) David Chase said that, despite all of his power and wealth, Tony Soprano is at heart a very insecure person.

(274) In the episode where Tony has food poisoning, Artie, understandably eager to absolve his own food from any blame, suggests that the Indian food Tony ate was the culprit because of the ghee. Ghee is a type of clarified butter that originated in South Asia. It is commonly used in Indian and Middle Eastern cooking, and is known for its rich, nutty flavor. Ghee is made by simmering butter to separate the milk solids and water, leaving behind only the pure butterfat.

(275) Michael Imperioli became a Buddhist in 2007.

(276) Tony watches the film It's a Gift in Long Term Parking. It's a Gift is a classic comedy film released in 1934 starring W.C. Fields.

(277) Puzzi is a reference to something that smells bad.

(278) It took about eighteen days to shoot one episode of The Sopranos.

(279) Uncle Junior is a fan of manicotti. Manicotti is a traditional Italian dish consisting of large pasta tubes filled with a mixture of ricotta cheese, spinach, and sometimes ground meat. The filled pasta tubes are then typically baked in a tomato sauce and topped with cheese before serving.

(280) Steven Van Zandt said he had never given any thought to being an actor until he was asked to be in The Sopranos.

(281) The surname Bompensiero means good thinker.

(282) James Gandolfini gave everyone on The Sopranos a watch when the show ended. It was inscribed - 'The Sopranos. 1997-2007. Rest in peace. Thank you. J.G.'

(283) Steven Soderbergh said that the two seminal shows in modern television history are Twin Peaks and The Sopranos and that anything 'good' today is standing on their shoulders.

(284) David Chase said that the reason he never did another television show after The Sopranos is that he has no interest in television shows!

(285) Braciole is mentioned in The Sopranos numerous times. Braciole is an Italian dish made with thinly pounded slices of meat, typically beef or pork, that are rolled up with a filling of breadcrumbs, cheese, herbs, and other ingredients. The rolls are then seared and simmered in a tomato sauce until tender.

(286) The Sopranos earned James Gandolfini three Emmy Awards and a Golden Globe for best actor.

(287) The tradition of the 'pork store' (that Tony and his crew often sit outside) is that there were no supermarkets in Italian-American immigrant communities. They preferred to get their food from traditional local shops.

(288) Michael Imperioli said he was thrilled to meet Steven Van Zandt on The Sopranos because he was a big Bruce Springsteen fan.

(289) Tony Soprano murders someone for the first time in episode five of season one. David Chase said that HBO were resistant to this because they feared that the character of Tony Soprano might lose sympathy with the audience. David had to

remind them that Tony is a mafia boss and a killer. He isn't a nice man!

(290) Ralphie Cifaretto has a secret tip to make good scrambled eggs - add sour cream.

(291) New Jersey was named after the Channel Island of Jersey. Jersey is located in the English Channel near the coast of Normandy. It is a self-governing British Crown dependency.

(292) In a 2024 interview, David Chase said he had only watched a few episodes of The Sopranos since it ended.

(293) Steven Van Zandt said in 2007 that he would have loved to have carried on making The Sopranos but they all accepted it was better to get out while the show was still good. Steven accepted too that James Gandolfini was pretty exhausted and deserved a break from the grueling schedule of being the lead in the show.

(294) Tony Soprano loves a good antipasto platter. An antipasto platter is a colorful and flavorful appetizer that typically consists of a variety of cured meats, cheeses, marinated vegetables, olives, and breadsticks. It is often served as a starter before a meal or as part of a charcuterie board.

(295) Christopher craves sugar when trying to quit drugs and takes back the Toblerone he gave Tony. Toblerone is a Swiss chocolate brand known for its distinctive triangular-shaped chocolate bars, which are made with honey and almond nougat.

(296) David Chase has confessed that he does get a bit tired of talking about The Sopranos sometimes because he usually gets asked the same questions all the time - like how did he get the idea for show and what did the ending mean etc.

(297) When the show was in production, James Gandolfini

would buy the crew sushi each Friday.

(298) Steven Van Zandt was wary of being in The Sopranos because he didn't want to feel like he was taking the job of an actor. David Chase therefore created the part of Silvio specially for him.

(299) David Chase said that he and James Gandolfini were barely talking and 'tired' of each other by the end of The Sopranos. They did though evidently patch things up because James took a role in David's 2012 film Not Fade Away.

(300) The characters in The Sopranos grapple with issues of identity, often struggling to reconcile their criminal personas with their roles as parents, spouses, and friends.

(301) Tim Van Patten directed 20 episodes of The Sopranos. In his younger years, as an actor, he played the obnoxious teen villain Peter Stegman in the exploitation film Class of 1984.

(302) Todd A. Kessler was a writer on seasons two and three of The Sopranos. HBO did not renew his contract for season four - which Kessler said was devastating. Kessler said that, when he heard the news, James Gandolfini took him out to dinner to try and cheer him up.

(303) Toni Kalem, who played Angie Bonpensiero, also wrote the season five episode All Happy Families.

(304) In the episode Funhouse, Tony has zucchini flowers. Zucchini flowers are the edible flowers that grow on zucchini plants. They have a subtle, squash-like flavor and are commonly used in cooking as a garnish or filling. They can be stuffed, battered and fried, or added to salads.

(305) James Manos Jr wrote five early episodes of The Sopranos. Among his later jobs were writing on The Shield and Dexter.

(306) David Chase named Join the Club and Mayham as his favorite Sopranos episodes. In these episodes Tony is fighting for his life and has strange coma dreams where is a heatings systems businessman named Kevin Finnerty. Kevin Finnerty represents what Tony Soprano might have been had he not been born into a life of crime. Tony's subconscious seems to perhaps assessing whether or not Tony might have been happier in a more normal sort of life.

(307) Terence Winter, who was a writer, director, and producer on The Sopranos would go on to create the highly regarded Boardwalk Empire - which starred Steve Buscemi.

(308) Carmine Lupertazzi Jr., known as Little Carmine, is the son of Carmine Lupertazzi Sr, the boss of the Lupertazzi crime family. Little Carmine is portrayed as a somewhat bumbling and ineffective leader, often making decisions that lead to chaos and conflict within the family.

(309) One of Carmela's specialties when it comes to baking is the ricotta pie. Ricotta pie is a traditional Italian dessert made with ricotta cheese, sugar, eggs, and sometimes additional flavorings such as citrus zest or chocolate chips. The mixture is poured into a pie crust and baked until the filling is set and the top is lightly golden brown

(310) Zeppole are traditional Italian pastries typically made during the feast of St. Joseph.

(311) Robert Loggia, who played Feech La Manna, had a bit of trouble learning his lines by all accounts. He was diagnosed with Alzheimer's disease about five years after appearing in The Sopranos.

(312) The Sopranos is often credited with kickstarting the anti-hero genre of modern television. Shows like Breaking Bad and The Shield, like The Sopranos, present a lead character who does terrible things - forcing the audience to question their feelings and loyalties.

(313) Paulie isn't too keen on the seafood themed pasta when he visits Italy and asks for 'macaroni and gravy' - a request which doesn't endear him to the locals.

(314) The American Italian Defence Association (AIDA) actually filed a lawsuit against The Sopranos - arguing that it was offensive to Italian-Americans. HBO and David Chase, not unreasonably, thought this was somewhat ridiculous. As they pointed out, no one could be stupid enough to believe that all Italian-Americans were mobsters or criminals just because of a TV show about the mafia.

(315) James Gandolfini had some drink and drugs problems when he appeared in The Sopranos. Some of those who worked on the show said he would sometimes turn up a bit the worse for wear and have to have several coffees to wake himself up.

(316) Ruffino Riserava Ducale Chianti Classico features quite a few times in The Sopranos. Ruffino Riserva Ducale Chianti Classico is a premium red wine from Tuscany, Italy. It is made from a blend of Sangiovese grapes grown in the renowned Chianti Classico region.

(317) David Chase said that with The Sopranos he wanted to show more of the mundane day to day life of the mob than you usually get in mafia films.

(318) In the scene where Bobby and Tony Soprano have a fight, Steve Schirripa and James Gandolofini did a lot of it without stuntmen to make it more realistic.

(319) Terence Winter said that an FBI agent told him that FBI employees would often talk about The Sopranos and debate how realistic it was.

(320) Vito Spatafore has a pool cue jammed in a part of his anatomy after his brutal death at the hands of Phil's crew for being gay. Joe Gannascoli, who played Vito, later allowed his

name to be used to promote a Rockwell Billiards pool stick but then withdrew after the Gay & Lesbian Alliance Against Defamation said this was in bad taste. "I had no idea it would create this sort of uproar," Gannascoli told the media. "I'm considering pulling all the pool cues. I'm a great supporter of the gay community."

(321) Eddie Falco said that one of her most vivid memories on The Sopranos was shooting a dinner scene at 3 in the morning and everyone trying to stay awake!

(322) They had to make fifteen dummy heads of Frank Vincent for Phil Leotardo's death scene.

(323) A lot of the writers on the show said that Christopher Moltisanti was a great character to write because Christopher thinks he is smart but he's actually quite dumb.

(324) The cast on The Sopranos would usually prepare for an episode by having a couple of read throughs together.

(325) The only voiceover scene in The Sopranos series proper is when we hear Vito's interior monologue when he is in hiding and working as a handyman. Vito is trying not to look at his watch and plainly struggling to adjust to life as an ordinary person - where you actually have to work a job and not just sit in a deckchair all day.

(326) In the episode Pine Barrens, Valery, the Russian who causes no end of trouble, is played by Vitali Baganov. Vitali Baganov is actually Russian in real life. He later appeared in the film Salt and the TV show The Americans.

(327) Frank Vincent said that during his time on The Sopranos he only saw David Chase on the set a couple of times.

(328) The script for Pine Barrens didn't mention snow. It simply started snowing shortly before shooting.

(329) Joe Gannascoli, who played Vito, had known John Costelloe - who played Vito's lover Johnny Cakes - for 20 years before The Sopranos.

(330) Eddie Falco said she rarely got recognized in public when The Sopranos was running because she looked very different to Carmela in real life.

(331) Johnny cakes are a type of flatbread or cornmeal pancake.

(332) Michael Imperioli said that Pine Barrens is so memorable because it is a darkly comic fish out of water yarn. Christopher and Paulie are completely out of their comfort zone out in the woods. They have no idea what they are doing.

(333) James Gandolfini said he was 'relived' when The Sopranos ended because he needed a rest. He said the show had changed his life but he was happy to move on.

(334) Frank Vincent said he was annoyed not to be in The Sopranos from the start because he worked with Dominic Chianese, Tony Sirico, and James Gandolfini before and had a lot of friends on the show.

(335) The scene where a couple of members of Tony's crew discover Vito dancing in a gay club in leathers was shot at a club on Queens. The extras were real nightclubbers.

(336) Dominic Chianese said the oversized glasses that Uncle Junior wore were great for helping him get into character.

(337) In the scene where Vito is killed, Phil Leotardo rather pointedly emerges from out of the closet!

(338) Tony Sirico said he was freezing shooting Pine Barrens because Paulie is not dressed for winter weather.

(339) The penultimate 1979 episode of The Rockford files,

written by David Chase is called Just a Coupla Guys. The episode is set in New Jersey and features a couple of 'mooks' who want to be mobsters. There is a mob boss called Tony who has a son named AJ and a cranky uncle. Sound familiar?

(340) Joe Gannascoli, who played Vito, was often in agony on The Sopranos because he had bad hips. He later had to have a double hip replacement.

(341) Salsiccia is an Italian sausage typically made from pork, seasoned with various herbs and spices such as fennel, garlic, and paprika.

(342) Terence Winter said that Tony Sirico and Paulie Walnuts were fairly similar. It was as if Tony was playing himself!

(343) Phil Leotardo spent 20 years in the can. Not that he ever mentions it!

(344) New Jersey is the most densely populated state in the United States.

(345) Jamie Lynn-Sigler combined her early years on The Sopranos with attending Jericho High School on Long Island.

(346) In the scene where Vito is killed, Phil Leotardo is seen gripping the bed. This seems to indicate that Phil is enjoying this murder and getting pleasure from it.

(347) The state capital of New Jersey is Trenton, but the largest city is Newark.

(348) Michael Imperioli said he knew Tony Sirico a little bit before The Sopranos and didn't actually like him. However, through their shared experiences on The Sopranos they became good friends.

(349) Joe Gannascoli said that one of the reasons why he proposed the storyline where Vito is revealed to be gay is that

he wanted more to do on the show.

(350) Steven Van Zandt said he would 'slump' down when he played Silvio to give the impression the character had the weight of the world on his shoulders and was carrying a few extra pounds.

(351) Alan Taylor said if The Sopranos was being made today they'd probably keep Christopher alive and do a Christopher & Paulie spin-off show!

(352) New Jersey is known as the Garden State due to its fertile soil and agricultural industry.

(353) Frank Vincent said David Chase told him the reason why he didn't cast him in The Sopranos from the start is that he felt was still too well known for Goodfellas and he wanted to go more for actors people wouldn't know so well.

(354) Nancy Marchand was (obviously) nothing like Livia in real life. The cast said she was very funny and nice.

(355) Over the course of the show, Bobby Baccalieri Jr is the only character who wins a fight with Tony. In fairness to Tony, he did get sucker punched!

(356) Federico Castelluccio, who played Furio, is a painter and artist in real life.

(357) Tony Sirico said that when he shot the episode Pine Barrens and Paulie loses a shoe in the snow, his foot got so cold he couldn't actually feel it anymore!

(358) Federico Castelluccio, who played Furio, said that at his Sopranos audition he improvised a few lines of profanity in Italian. He thinks this is what got him the job.

(359) David Chase said a big theme of The Sopranos is consumerism. The mobsters want the nice things in life - be it

electronic goods, the best food, fancy cars etc.

(360) Vincent Curatola, who played Johnny Sack, said he didn't want to go to his Sopranos audition because he assumed the show would be like Saturday Night Fever or a music themed series. His agent managed to persuade him to attend.

(361) Terence Winter, who created Boardwalk Empire, said they did think of James Gandolfini as the lead of that show but in the end they decided it was too soon after The Sopranos. Audiences would struggle to see him as another character and Gandolfini was also highly unlikely to want to plunge into another television show. Steve Buscemi was therefore cast.

(362) James Gandolfini would sometimes put a rock in his shoe as an irritation to get into character for scenes where Tony is in a bad mood or angry.

(363) Vincent Curatola, who played Johnny Sack, said he was only initially hired to do one episode. He ended up appearing in 33 episodes in all.

(364) Steve Schirripa said the Bobby/Tony fight was designed to be much more realistic than your typical TV/Hollywood fight scene. Steve said it was basically two fat out of shape men wrestling one another!

(365) David Chase said that it was for the best that his original idea of having Steven Van Zandt play Tony Soprano didn't come to pass. David thinks the show would have been too comedic with Steven in that part.

(366) When they did location shooting for The Sopranos they had to pay the The Irish American Association of Kearny, New Jersey, money to take down an Irish flag so that an Italian one could be put up as a backdrop.

(367) Tony Sirico said that a scene explaining what happened to the Russian who Paulie and Christopher lost in Pine

Barrens was written but never filmed. Tony said the scene would have had Christopher and Paulie running into the Russian but seeing that he had brain damage from the bullet and didn't remember anything.

(368) Michael Imperioli said he'd never heard of David Chase when he did his Sopranos audition.

(369) Edie Falco shot a cameo as Carmela for The Many Saints of Newark but it was cut out. We do briefly see the young Carmela in the prequel though - played by Lauren DiMario.

(370) In 2002 it was reported that the University of Calgary in Canada were offering a film studies/literature course where students could study the themes of The Sopranos.

(371) Edie Falco said that, unlike Carmela, she can't cook at all in real life.

(372) James Gandolfini said he didn't like the way The Sopranos ended when he first saw it but upon reflection he thought it was perfect.

(373) Lorraine Bracco said she was broke when she got the part of Dr Melfi due to a custody battle and a tax bill. Her early years on the show saw her salary go towards paying this off.

(374) Steve Van Zandt said that when he went for his Sopranos audition, James Gandolfini was one of the people sitting outside waiting to be called.

(375) Tony Soprano's full name is Anthony John "Tony" Soprano, Sr.

(376) When the show was in its pomp, James Gandolfini would sometimes be irritated when fans wanted him to sign autographs as 'Tony Soprano' rather than his real name.

(377) Edie Falco said she tried watching The Sopranos a few

years back but found it too depressing because of James Gandolofini's passing.

(378) One reason why a number of Sopranos fans were irritated by The Many Saints of Newark is that the marketing led one to believe this was a Tony Soprano origin story and yet it wasn't that at all. Tony played a surprisingly minor role in the story.

(379) The Sopranos was budgeted at $2 million an episode when it began. This eventually went up to $6 million an episode.

(380) Vincent Curatola, who played Johnny Sack, said he knew James Gandolfini before The Sopranos because a lot of the New York actors would eat at the same places.

(381) Paulie Gualtieri is fond of weight lifting.

(382) Johnny Sack was named after Sac's Place - an eatery in Queens that The Sopranos writers would frequent. Sac's Place would send food to The Sopranos set for the cast and crew at lunch.

(383) When the last parts of The Sopranos went out, a lot of fans on the forums complained about the Vito/Johnny Cakes storyline because they felt the show was wasting valueable time on this supporting character when there weren't that many episodes left.

(384) The house used for Uncle Junior's home was a four-bedroom property in Newark's Forest Hills. The house went up for sale in 2023 with an asking price of $585,000.

(385) Drea de Matteo said that David Chase didn't think she was Italian enough to play Adriana at first but he obviously came around in the end.

(386) Robert Iler was twelve years-old when he was cast as

Tony Soprano's son.

(387) The trouble that Paulie and Christopher have with the Russian in Pine Barrens is largely Paulie's fault because he unnecessarily insults Valery quite a lot when in his apartment - despite the fact that Valery is being perfectly civil and even offers them a drink!

(388) Gogoots means squash.

(389) Tony Sirico also auditioned for the part of Salvatore 'Big Pussy' Bonpensiero before he was assigned the part of Paulie.

(390) When they shot a scene on The Sopranos on location they often had onlookers but they managed to avoid major spoilers leaking out. In those days there were no drones or smart phones so it was a bit easier to shoot in privacy than it is today.

(391) Michael Imperioli famously played Spider - the kid serving the drinks at the poker game that Joe Pesci shoots in the foot and then murders in Goodfellas.

(392) Chiacchierone means someone who talks a lot.

(393) The cast on The Sopranos would get their scripts at the same time - presumably to lessen the chances of spoilers leaking out.

(394) Joe Pantoliano described Ralphie as being like a Shakespearian villain.

(395) Paulie Gualtieri is what you could describe as a germophobe. He's very strict on hygiene. This is a trait Tony Sirico shared.

(396) Robert Iler said it was weird when The Sopranos ended because he was now unemployed for the first time in his young life!

(397) The diner scene which ended The Sopranos wasn't the last scene to be shot. They still had other scenes to shoot after getting that one in the can.

(398) Michael Imperioli said that when he did his Sopranos audition David Chase kept asking him to do it differently. This made Michael (wrongly) presume that his audition was terrible.

(399) Ralph Cifaretto turns up in the show as if the characters all know him and he's always been around - even though we (the audience) haven't met him. This is explained away in the show by Ralphie having been in Miami.

(400) Vincent Curatola, who played Johnny Sack, said that as a consequence of being in The Sopranos he did become 'picky' about taking new acting roles. After being in The Sopranos literally everything felt like a step down.

(401) The part of Carmela Soprano was the last to be cast because they had trouble finding an actress who they thought was right.

(402) David Chase said it was just a coincidence that so many people from Goodfellas got cast in The Sopranos. They were simply the best people for the job at the auditions.

(403) Jamie Lynn-Sigler has a Cuban mother and a Jewish father. She said she was often assumed to be of Italian descent in real life so it wasn't too much of a stretch to cast her in The Sopranos as the daughter of Italian-Americans.

(404) Frankie Valli initially auditioned for the part of Beansie Gaeta. Beansie was the poor man left paralyzed by Richie. Paul Herman played Beansie in the end.

(405) Drea de Matteo said she had a crush on James Gandolfini when she was in The Sopranos.

(406) Michael Imperioli said he knew about a year in advance that Christopher was going to die. He didn't mind though because he was in the show up to fairly near the end.

(407) Jerry Adler was only supposed to appear in one episode as Hesh but it became a larger role in the end.

(408) The late Robert Pastorelli auditioned to play Richie Aprile. Robert Pastorelli was best known for his role as Eldin Bernecky on the TV show Murphy Brown. He also appeared in several films, including Sister Act 2: Back in the Habit and Eraser. Pastorelli also played the lead in an American remake of the British drama show Cracker. One of the people he beat to get this part in Cracker was a certain James Gandolfini.

(409) The cast on The Sopranos said you could smell Tony Sirico coming a mile off because he always carried a bottle of Calvin Klein's Obsession so that he smelled nice.

(410) A common complaint of The Many Saints of Newark is that the film could never quite decide what it wanted to be.

(411) At the start of The Sopranos, Tony and his crew watch a former criminal on television talk about the decline of the mob and make light of this as they count money. However, Tony knows there is truth in the analysis. He tells Dr Melfi that he feels as if he has come into something right at the end.

(412) One of David Chase's stipulations for The Sopranos was that it had to be shot on location in authentic New Jersey locations.

(413) Sopranos costume designer Juliet Polcsa said a lot of the stores where she bought clothes for the characters don't exist anymore.

(414) Drea de Matteo went from The Sopranos straight into the Friends sitcom spin-off Joey. Joey was axed after two seasons.

(415) Steve Schirripa said his agent advised him to turn down The Sopranos because his part seemed minor and the money wasn't great at first. Luckily for Steve he ignored that advice.

(416) Michael Imperioli said that at the start of the show he didn't have the faintest idea if The Sopranos would find an audience or be watched by anyone.

(417) Soppressata is a type of Italian salami that is made from coarsely ground pork and flavored with various spices, such as garlic, black pepper, and paprika

(418) Janice Soprano is a famously terrible cook in the show.

(419) Tony Soprano is partial to Glenlivet. Glenlivet is a renowned Scottish distillery that produces single malt Scotch whisky. It is located in the Speyside region of Scotland and is known for its smooth and fruity whiskies.

(420) Michael Imperioli turned down a part in the Woody Allen film Celebrity to do The Sopranos pilot. That turned out to be a very shrewd decision.

(421) Paulie likes white slip on loafer shoes. He thinks shoelaces are unhygienic because they gather dirt and germs.

(422) According to his son Michael, James Gandolfini had a special soundproofed room in his house he would go to when he wanted to run through his lines.

(423) Jon Favreau made a cameo in The Sopranos as a director. The part played by Favreau was intended for Quentin Tarantino but Tarantino was unavailable.

(424) 'Whack' means to kill or murder someone.

(425) Furio is a rarity in that he left the show without being murdered!

(426) Jamie-Lynn Sigler and Robert Iler had to have a tutor and school classes on the set of The Sopranos when they first started on the show.

(427) David Chase said that if The Sopranos had been purely about the mafia it probably wouldn't have worked because the mob genre has been done many times in film and television. He felt the insight into Tony's family life and therapy was much needed.

(428) James Gandolfini said he was surprised to be cast as the lead in a television show because he assumed HBO would want more of a George Clooney type.

(429) The character Little Carmine Lupertazzi was partly based on George W. Bush in the way that he will get phrases wrong and give the impression of not being the sharpest knife in the drawer.

(430) The character 'Little' Carmine Lupertazzi was supposed to be a huge overweight man - which made his nickname rather ironic. In the end though they changed their plans and cast the normal sized Ray Abruzzo.

(431) Father Phil is portrayed by Michael Santoro in the pilot. Paul Schulze took over this role in the actual series.

(432) The singer Madonna was considered for the Karen Hill part played by Lorraine Bracco in Goodfellas.

(433) Tony Sirico was in his thirties when he began his first steps to being an actor.

(434) The 'goomahs' (mistresses) of the mobsters in The Sopranos are all a lot younger than their wives.

(435) Tony Sirico said in an interview that the reason Pussy got bumped off is that Vincent Pastore kept asking for time off to do other things.

(436) David Chase said he didn't want to cast someone too conventionally handsome as Tony Soprano because Tony's allure is his power and wealth - not his looks.

(437) James Gandolfini's first credit was in an obscure low-budget 1987 horror film called Shock! Shock! Shock! He played an orderly in the film.

(438) Tony's crew have their egos dented when they visit Italy and see that the mob over there have much more lavish and high class lifestyles than they do.

(439) Vincent Curatola, who played Johnny Sack, was in his forties when he started acting.

(440) The 'wings' of white hair on the side of Paulie's head became more exaggerated as the show went on.

(441) Nick Lowe's The Beast in Me is the song playing at the end of the pilot.

(442) Joe Pantoliano was one of the villains in the cult adventure film The Goonies.

(443) Martin Scorsese makes a 'cameo' in an early Sopranos episode but it wasn't really Scorsese - just a stand-in.

(444) Pussy disappeared at the end of season one. David Chase later admitted that he had no idea where the character was! He had to figure something out.

(445) The thing that distinguished The Sopranos from Goodfellas and The Godfather is that it wasn't a period piece in any way. It was set firmly in the present day. Of course, when people now and in the future watch The Sopranos it WILL became a period piece from their perspective!

(446) Vito appears in weight loss commercials in season six. This is because Joe Gannascoli had lap-band surgery in real

life and lost about 130 pounds. Lap-band surgery, also known as gastric banding, is a type of weight loss surgery that involves placing a silicone band around the upper part of the stomach to create a small pouch. This restricts the amount of food the stomach can hold, leading to a feeling of fullness with less food and ultimately promoting weight loss.

(447) Tony Sirico apparently used to do martial arts in real life.

(448) Scarface (the 1983 version) is mentioned in the first season. Robert Loggia, who later played Feech in the show, was actually in this film.

(449) The episode Pine Barrens led some viewers to assume that a mob war between Tony Soprano and the Russians was on the way. David Chase patently wasn't interested in that though.

(450) When the first episode of The Sopranos went out Facebook and Twitter had yet to be invented. There wasn't even Myspace yet either.

(451) Robert Iler said it doesn't bother him when people still ask about The Sopranos all the time. He said he is grateful for being part of the show.

(452) James Gandolfini was paid one million dollars an episode in the last season.

(453) One of the writers on the show said Tony Sirico would wake up three hours before he was due to come in for the morning shoot and spend those three hours doing his hair!

(454) David Chase had cameos in Commendatori, Luxury Lounge, and The Test Dream.

(455) Tony Sirico said that The Sopranos and Paulie Walnuts was the show and role he'd been waiting for his whole life.

(456) David Chase said he didn't much like the episode Commendatori where Tony went to Italy. He didn't think it worked very well.

(457) According to online sources, James Gandolfini had a net wealth of $70 million when he died.

(458) In 2024, the cast and crew from The Sopranos had a reunion dinner at Da Nico, a restaurant on Mulberry Street, Little Italy. Baked Ziti was the main dish on the menu.

(459) Maria Salandra was the manicurist on The Sopranos. Maria came up with the nail designs for characters like Adriana and Carmela.

(460) The website Ranker has The Sopranos as the eighth most 'binge worthy' show of all time. Game of Thrones took first place.

(461) Corey Stoll plays Junior Soprano in The Many Saints of Newark. Stoll does a pretty good Dominic Chianese impression.

(462) Sentimental Education (the name of a Sopranos episode) is a novel written by Gustave Flaubert, first published in 1869. It tells the story of a young man named Frederic Moreau, who falls in love with a married woman named Madame Arnoux and becomes entangled in various romantic and social affairs.

(463) The cast of The Sopranos said it was sort of weird that Lorraine Bracco was one of the stars of the show and yet apart from James Gandolfini no one had any scenes with her!

(464) David Chase said that the 9/11 attack on New York bled into the show and made it more downbeat.

(465) In the episode For All Debts Public and Private, Tony Soprano is watching the film Rio Bravo. Rio Bravo is a 1959

American Western film directed by Howard Hawks and starring John Wayne, Dean Martin, Ricky Nelson, and Angie Dickinson. The film follows a sheriff and his ragtag group of allies as they try to keep a dangerous prisoner from being freed by his powerful brother.

(466) It is suggested that Phil Leotardo either had homosexual experiences in prison or was the victim of sexual abuse. There is his obsession with Vito's sexuality and also a moment where he gets annoyed because there are male bodybuilders on television.

(467) Jamie-Lynn Sigler said wedding scenes in The Sopranos were quite dull to shoot because you had to wait around for hours in costume and probably get not much more than a line to say.

(468) David Chase said it was quite difficult to contact Steven Van Zandt to ask him to audition for The Sopranos. He's obviously not an easy man to get on the phone.

(469) Robert Iler has (modestly) said he was the worst actor in The Sopranos.

(470) Shooting the table scenes outside the pork store for the show were difficult because there were a lot of onlookers and autograph hunters.

(471) AJ had his eyebrows shaved off by friends in The Sopranos. In reality, Robet Iler didn't have to shave his eyebrows off. It was done by a make-up artist.

(472) Tony Soprano has a gambling addiction in the show.

(473) Frank Ferrara was a stunt double for James Gandolfini/Tony Soprano. Frank Ferrara was a stunt co-ordinator on many big movies.

(474) In the season six scene where Phil has crashed his car

and Tony roughs him up, Steve Buscemi was in the back of the car directing the scene.

(475) In decades past the mob had many tentacles in areas like showbusiness and sports.

(476) The television show that Christopher is watching in For All Debts Public and Private is Magnum P.I with Tom Selleck.

(477) Matt Servitto, who played Special Agent Dwight Harris, said he is still recognized from the show and asked for autographs.

(478) The Bada Bing! strip joint is owned and run by Silvio.

(479) Christopher shooting a bakery worker in the foot is an obvious shout out to Michael Imperioli's role as Spider in Goodfellas - where his character got shot in the foot.

(480) Steven Spielberg said he did a Sopranos rewatch during the pandemic.

(481) David Chase said that consumerism as distraction is a key theme in The Sopranos. The characters use money, food, and material possessions as a distraction from their problems.

(482) Tony Sirico was 55 when he was cast in The Sopranos. He truly loved the show and the limelight it gave him because it came later in his life and he appreciated it all the more for that.

(483) Angelo Massagli, who played one of Bobby Baccalieri's kids, later got a law degree in real life.

(484) Robert Iler has admitted that he was pretty lazy and shallow compared to other Sopranos cast members. Whenever there was a hiatus in the show the other actors would look for a play to do but all Robert wanted to do was go to nightclubs and get drunk.

(485) Veal pizzaiola is sometimes on the menu in the Soprano home. Veal pizzaiola is a traditional Italian dish made with thinly sliced veal simmered in a sauce made of tomatoes, herbs, garlic, and olive oil.

(486) VirtualCons' staged an event An Evening at Tony's in 2021. Guests spent an evening at the real house used for Tony and Carmela's house in the show. Aida Turturro was among the cast members who attended and admitted she got quite emotional being there again.

(487) Alec Baldwin is a big Sopranos fan and said he unsuccessfully lobbied to get on the show.

(488) The real location for Ooh-Fa Pizza & Restaurant was Ralph Piccolo's Pizza in Paterson.

(489) Edie Falco had third billing in the show despite having the second largest part.

(490) Michael Imperioli was 31 when he filmed The Sopranos pilot. Christopher is supposed to be in his mid twenties.

(491) Drea de Matteo later played Wendy Teller on FX's Sons of Anarchy.

(492) Two different child actors played Vito Spatafore Jr - Frank Borrelli and Brandon Hannan.

(493) Steve Schirripa said he tried to avoid doing mob movies after The Sopranos because most of them are terrible.

(494) The Many Saints of Newark ends with the theme song from The Sopranos.

(495) Tony Lip, who played Carmine Lupertazzi, said he was a bit typecast as an actor because everyone always said he looked like a mafia boss in real life!

(496) One of the most entertaining (if fanciful) Sopranos fan theories is that Adriana somehow survived being killed in the woods by Silvio and was the person who hired the man to shoot Tony in the diner in the last ever scene!

(497) There was a Sopranos official pinball machine released by Stern Pinball in 2005.

(498) The Many Saints of Newark has a fairly mediocre audience score of 59% on Rotten Tomatoes.

(499) A lot of The Sopranos cast did casino appearances during the show.

(500) Tony Soprano wears a Saint Christopher medallion.

(501) New Jersey is known for its coastline, including popular beach towns such as Atlantic City, Cape May, and Asbury Park.

(502) The younger Livia is played by Laila Robins in two Sopranos episodes and by Laurie Williams in another.

(503) The Sopranos has been praised for its blend of crime drama and family saga.

(504) The last season of The Sopranos was an intense production because at one point they shot nine episodes in nine months.

(505) Bobby's daughter Sophia Baccalieri was played by two different child actors - Lexie Sperduto and Miryam Coppersmith.

(506) David Chase regretted killing Philly Parisi because he liked Dan Grimaldi's performance. This is why they got Grimaldi back at Philly's twin Patsy.

(507) Tony Blundetto's mother, Quintina Blundetto, was played by two different actresses - Barbara Andres and Rae

Allen.

(508) Lorraine Bracco once worked as a fashion model for Jean-Paul Gaultier.

(509) Tony Sirico had over 80 credits in his acting career.

(510) Aida Turturro majored in theater at State University of New York.

(511) Tony Soprano's grandfather was a stone mason.

(512) The real location for the Averna Social Club was the Mulberry Street Bar in Little Italy.

(513) Pizza Land on the Belleville Turnpike, which features in the titles, doesn't just serve pizza. They also do sandwiches, pasta, chicken, onion rings, and more.

(514) Paulie is rather bewildered when he is served black pasta in Italy. Black pasta is a type of pasta that is made with squid ink, giving it a dark black color.

(515) The word "mafia" may have its roots in the Arabic word "mahias," meaning bold man.

(516) Mangia means eat!

(517) Robert Iler said he was quite annoyed when he got cast in the pilot for The Sopranos because it meant he was going to miss summer camp!

(518) Mick Jagger and The Rolling Stones were all huge Sopranos fans.

(519) Robert Iler said that when he was kid on The Sopranos his big celebrity crush was the actress Jennifer Love Hewitt. Sadly though for Robert she was never in The Sopranos.

(520) Capisce means do you understand?

(521) The great Muhammad Ali visited the Sopranos studio when the show was in production and had a photo taken with James Gandolfini.

(522) Tony Lip, who played Carmine Lupertazzi, was behind a cookbook in which some of the Sopranos cast shared their favorite recipes.

(523) Robert Iler said that he doesn't get drunk or take drugs anymore. He's calmed down a bit with with age.

(524) During the run of The Sopranos, HBO had an exclusive deal with David Chase which prevented him writing a show for another network.

(525) Robert Iler said that at his Catholic confirmation, James Gandolfini and Tony Sirico both attended and gave him a big envelope full of money!

(526) Julianna Margulies played Julianna Skiff in the show - the character being someone who attracts the romantic interest of both Christopher and Tony. Margulies said she was going to turn down the part because she didn't like the idea of playing a drug addict but her actor friend Griffin Dunne told she would be crazy to turn the show down.

(527) Drea de Matteo was strangely absent from the Talking Sopranos podcast hosted by Michael Imperioli and Steve Schirripa. Given that they had a guest each week from the show you'd have assumed that Drea de Matteo would have been one of the first people they booked.

(528) Vincent Curatola was also a notable absentee from the Talking Sopranos podcast. There was speculation that the left leaning Michael Imperioli didn't want him on because Curatola is very conservative (if his social media is anything to go by) but that could just be speculation.

(529) Joe Gannascoli (Vito) was also absent from the Talking Sopranos podcast. Gannascoli said he wouldn't be listening to it - which suggests he isn't on great terms with Michael Imperioli and Steve Schirripa.

(530) Drea de Matteo only mentioned the names Robert Iler and Vincent Curatola (Johnny Sack) when asked which Sopranos cast members she is still in touch with.

(531) Jamie-Lynn Sigler said she never knew much about her scenes until she arrived at the studio and would usually learn her lines at the last minute.

(532) If you are one of those fans who think Tony died at the end of the show then things look bleak for Carmela and her kids. Tony is dead, Bobby is dead, Christopher is dead, Silvio is in a coma. Paulie is still alive but Paulie doesn't like Carmela very much and is unlikely to be trusted when it comes to getting Tony's money to her.

(533) The premiere for season five of The Sopranos was held at New York's Radio City Music Hall.

(534) Satin Dolls, which doubled as the Bada Bing! strip joint, cashed in on its association with the show by selling Sopranos souvenirs and merch.

(535) Tony Lip, who played Carmine Lupertazzi, was born Frank Anthony Vallelonga. He appeared in both The Godfather and Goodfellas.

(536) Robert Iler said he had never seen The Godfather or Goodfellas when he was working on the early seasons of The Sopranos. When the cast heard this they told him to watch them - so he did. To be fair to him he was only about thirteen at the time.

(537) Tony Sirico was living with his mother when he was cast in The Sopranos. The show was a timely boost to his flagging

career.

(538) Denise Borino-Quinn, who played Ginny Sacrimoni, worked in a law firm in New Brunswick, New Jersey away from the show.

(539) Robert Iler said that when people ask him about Sopranos episodes he usually has no idea what they are talking about because he only watched a couple of them.

(540) Uncle Junior actor Dominic Chianese lives in England these days. He actually met up with Alabama 3 in London. Alabama 3, as we noted, wrote the song's theme song.

(541) Matt Servitto, who played Special Agent Dwight Harris, said he never thought HBO would commit to The Sopranos because the show was so daring. He was delighted to be proven wrong.

(542) David Chase said that Goodfellas was the biggest influence on The Sopranos in the way that it was both brutal and funny - often at the same time.

(543) We sometimes hear songs by Steven van Zandt on the radio in The Sopranos.

(544) One of the strippers at Bada Bing! was played by the wrestling star Elektra. Elektra's real name is Donna Adamo.

(545) In the episode Christopher, Tony refers to the film High Noon. High Noon is a 1952 American Western film directed by Fred Zinnemann and starring Gary Cooper and Grace Kelly. The film tells the story of a town marshal who is forced to face a gang of outlaws alone when no one in the town is willing to help him.

(546) One of Tony's cars in the show is a 1999 Chevy Suburban.

(547) Al Gore was given a copy of the final Sopranos episode by HBO to watch on his plane.

(548) It is probably fair to say that Dr Melfi becomes a less important character as the show goes on.

(549) Bobby Baccalieri Jr's hobby is model toy trains. This gives us an insight into his character. At heart he is quite an innocent and gentle man. He isn't really cut out for the mob.

(550) Paulie and Christopher have a love/hate relationship in the show. Paulie is loyal to Christopher and they go through much together but Paulie is also jealous of Christopher's youth and closeness to Tony - which leads to Paulie being petty at times in his treatment of Christopher.

(551) Dominic Chianese said he would even wear Uncle Junior's spectacles at the rehearsals to get into character.

(552) A common question people have about Frank Sinatra concern his links to the mafia. Was Sinatra connected to the mob? Well, yes and no seems to be the answer. Sinatra was not a mobster but he was friendly with mafia bosses and associates, this stretching back to his early days in New Jersey. Lucky Luciano arranged for him to perform at many of his parties in Havana, Sinatra even allegedly being at the 1947 Havana Conference. Luciano also borrowed 2 million dollars from Sinatra at one point. Sinatra did many concerts on behest of the mob.

In 1976 Sinatra was photographed posing with mob bosses and personalities like Paul Castellano, Joe Gambino, and 'Jimmy the Weasel' Fratianno at the Westchester Premier Theater, NYC. Sinatra's daughter Tina said that her father used mob ties to help boost a young John F Kennedy in politics. It is often alleged that Sinatra used the mafia to get a part in From Here to Eternity. There is some debate over this claim. What is certainly true is that Sinatra knew powerful mafia figures and seemed to like associating with them at social functions or events. He did concerts for them and it seems likely the mafia and Sinatra did each other a few favors.

(553) Frank Vincent had to be careful not to exert himself in season six because he'd just had open heart surgery.

(554) Edie Falco brought her dog to the set in the last season. The dog ruined a few takes by barking and wandering into shots.

(555) James Gandolfini's father had a cameo as a butcher in the episode Fortunate Son.

(556) The Pizza Land store you see in the titles was never used for filming in the show but some of the cast did visit and try the pizza.

(557) Rober Iler said that he went on a 'bender' to Las Vegas during The Sopranos and couldn't do any scenes when he came back because he'd lost his voice.

(558) David Chase said he never started plotting out the next season of The Sopranos until HBO had confirmed that they wanted another season - despite the fact that HBO were hardly likely to cancel their most popular show!

(559) In the episode Cold Stones, Vito's murder is compared to that of Ramon Navarro. Ramon Navarro was a Chilean actor renowned for his roles in silent films during the Golden Age of Hollywood. He was tragically murdered in 1968 in his home in Los Angeles. The notion that Navarro had a strange or sordid death is an urban myth which originates from the book Hollywood Babylon. Hollywood Babylon is a trashy cult book about Hollywood scandals and 'secrets' from the 1900s onwards. It was written by 'experimental' underground filmmaker Kenneth Anger and first published in French in 1959. Many of its claims have been completely debunked and the book created a number of urban myths that have no basis whatsoever in reality - like the story that the silent film actress

Clara Bow once slept with an entire American Football team.

(560) David Chase said he never found the character Salvatore "Big Pussy" Bonpensiero that interesting.

(561) The film Ginny Sacrimoni is watching in The Weight is Penny Serenade. Penny Serenade is a 1941 American melodrama film starring Irene Dunne and Cary Grant.

(562) The title Mr Ruggerio's Neighborhood is a riff on the kids TV show Mister Rogers' Neighborhood.

(563) David Chase said that the story dictated which character would die. How popular a character was did not come into it.

(564) Annabella Sciorra was considered for the part of Janice before playing Gloria.

(565) When they shot the episode Pine Barrens, Tony Sirico didn't like the pillows in his hotel so he got someone to fetch the pillows from his house.

(566) Paulie refers to Meadow's boyfriend Finn as Shaggy. Shaggy is a character from the cartoon Scooby-Doo.

(567) Carmela finds the book The Letters of Abelard and Heloise in Sentimental Education. The Letters of Abelard and Heloise is a collection of correspondences between the 12th-century French philosopher Peter Abelard and his student and lover Heloise.

(568) Robert Iler said he can't remember much about the last season of The Sopranos because he was partying so much.

(569) When he got the part of Tony Soprano, James Gandolfini put on some weight because he thought a mob boss would probably be carrying a few extra pounds.

(570) Those on the show said there was a thin line between

Tony Sirico and Paulie Walnuts. He would come out of the wardrobe and make-up departments basically looking the same as he did on the street!

(571) David Chase decided to do eight extra episodes when season six was already filming. He obviously consulted the cast to make sure they were happy to do this.

(572) Drea de Matteo was in 48 episodes as Adriana.

(573) James Gandolfini was billed as Jim Gandolfini when he began his acting career.

(574) The pilot for The Sopranos has some voiceover narration. This is something that was wisely jettisoned in the series.

(575) James Gandolfini was 6 feet tall. They make him look much bigger than that in The Sopranos though because Tony often seems to dwarf other characters in scenes.

(576) One of Tony Sirico's earliest roles was in an episode of the police show Kojak.

(577) In the first episode, Carmela tells Meadow that she can't lie and cheat and ignore rules she doesn't like. The irony of this lecture is not lost on the audience because this is exactly what her husband Tony does as a mobster!

(578) For the food scenes, Edie Falco had a trick of putting some gum in the side of her moth so it looked like she was eating something when in fact she was not.

(579) Edie Falco was on $500,000 an episode by the end of The Sopranos.

(580) The statues and art pieces featured in the show carry symbolic meanings related to power, legacy, and morality.

(581) When the first episode of The Sopranos went out, Bill Clinton was still in the White House.

(582) The horse Pie-O-My serves as a symbol of Tony's desire for something pure and innocent in his life.

(583) Tony loses telephone contact with Paulie and Christopher in Pine Barrens. It was much harder to get a signal in rural areas in those days.

(584) The themes of loyalty and betrayal are prominent throughout the series, highlighting the complexities of trust and allegiance within the criminal underworld.

(585) We see Tony watching the 1993 film The Fugitive in The Sopranos. Joe Pantoliano was in this film.

(586) The Sopranos delves into the complexities of identity, particularly in the context of being a mobster, a family member, and a member of a particular community.

(587) David Chase said he went into a bit of a panic when HBO asked for The Sopranos to become a full series because it meant he would now have to come up with plots beyond his basic 'mobster goes to therapy' idea.

(588) In a Huffington Post article in 2010, The Sopranos was named the best show of the decade. Deadwood and The Wire were second and third.

(589) Tony beats up Ralph Cifaretto after Ralph kills the young pregnant stripper Tracee. Ralph is quick to point out this against mafia code because he is a made man and can't be touched. Under the mafia code, Tony WOULD have been permitted to beat up or kill Ralph if Tracee was a blood relative of his or his mistress or wife.

(590) David Chase said that AJ and Meadow were not written not to be 'cute or funny' or cool because he wanted them to

seem like realistic annoying kids and not your standard Hollywood teenagers.

(591) Johnny Sack wasn't seen much early on but became a more prominent character as the show progressed.

(592) The show's nonlinear storytelling allowed for flashbacks and dream sequences.

(593) Naples is a city in southern Italy, known for its rich history, art, architecture, and cuisine. It is located on the Bay of Naples near Mount Vesuvius, the volcano that famously destroyed the ancient Roman city of Pompeii.

(594) The hotel that Tony Soprano stayed in when he went to Naples is the Hotel Excelsior.

(595) Meadow attends Columbia. Columbia University is a private Ivy League research university located in New York City. It was established in 1754 and is one of the oldest universities in the United States.

(596) Meadow has a bit of a shock when she goes to Columbia University because the other students are just as smart as she is and come from upper class wealthy families. Meadow comes from a wealthy family too but her father is basically an uneducated mobster who gained his money through crime and murder.

(597) Michael Imperioli said he did research on heroin and drug addiction to play Christopher. His acting when Christopher is drug addled is very convincing.

(598) The acting boss of the Zucca Camorra Family in Naples is Annalisa Zucca (née Vittorio). This character was played by the Swiss born actress Sofia Milos.

(599) David Chase later said he thought Sofia Milos was miscast as Annalisa Zucca and wasn't very convincing as a

mafia boss/wife.

(600) Like Meadow at Columbia, AJ has a similar reality check when it turns out his girlfriend's family is much wealthier than his own. Tony Soprano has a comfortable life but he isn't among the mega rich in America.

(601) There was no official product placement on The Sopranos but it is noticeable that a lot of the same brands feature. Everyone has a Phillips television, Diet Coke is everywhere etc.

(602) Christopher wants to cast Sir Ben Kingsley in his film Cleaver but has to settle for Daniel Baldwin.

(603) Food in The Sopranos often represents family, tradition, and power. Food also serves as a way to showcase status and power within the criminal organization, with lavish meals and elaborate feasts used to demonstrate wealth and influence. Certain foods and dishes serve as symbols of cultural heritage.

(604) In the last episode AJ talks about being a helicopter pilot for Donald Trump.

(605) Silvio Dante's character was based on a character in a story Steven Van Zandt had written. He obviously showed this story to David Chase.

(606) David Chase said that many of Livia's cutting and sarcastic remarks were based on things his mother said.

(607) The picture on the wall in the Bada Bing! office is a police mugshot of a young Frank Sinatra.

(608) The series' final season was split into two parts, with the second half airing after a hiatus, building anticipation for its conclusion.

(609) Tony Sirico would instruct other actors on the set of The

Sopranos as if he was the director! He was very enthusiastic about the show.

(610) The Sopranos was unusual in that it didn't have a music composer or music score. It was all source music or soundtrack songs.

(611) When his career hit a barren spot in the early 1980s, David Proval was an acting coach for a time. He was actually the acting coach for Eddie Murphy in Murphy's first film - 48 Hrs.

(612) David Chase said he tried to approach The Sopranos as if each episode was a mini movie all of its own.

(613) Max Casella, who played Benny Fazio, was also considered for the parts of Matt Bevilaqua and Jackie Aprile, Jr.

(614) The Sopranos was a critical and commercial success throughout its run.

(615) Vincent Pastore said he was very sad when his character Pussy was killed off in The Sopranos but he did quickly find a silver lining in that his Sopranos fame led him to being offered more parts in movies.

(616) There was what is known as a 'writer's room' on The Sopranos. They all contributed and came up with ideas.

(617) David Chase said that they felt a lot of pressure making season two because of all the critical acclaim of season one. They had a lot of expectations to live up to.

(618) The character of Tony Soprano has been ranked among the greatest television characters in history.

(619) David Chase said he always saw The Sopranos as a comedy drama. Even in the midst of the terrible things the

characters do there is always humor.

(620) Oksana Lada, who played Tony's 'goomah' Irina Peltsin, said she thinks that Irina just wants to find a man to marry so she will feel protected and loved.

(621) Steven Van Zandt was in the Martin Scorsese film The Irishman. He played Jerry Vale. Jerry Vale was an American singer known for his romantic ballads and smooth vocal style.

(622) David Chase said that he doesn't think that AJ or Meadow will have anything to do with crime or the mob in their later years. He thinks both became ordinary 'civilians' with normal jobs.

(623) Oogatz is a term used in Italian slang to mean "nothing" or "worthless."

(624) The film director Mike Nichols turned down the part of Dr Krakower (the therapist that Dr Melfi advises Carmela to talk to). Sully Boyar played this part.

(625) David Chase said none of the mobsters in The Sopranos are based on people he has met. They are all purely fictional. He said the family of Tony Soprano is though sort of based on some of his own relatives - especially Livia.

(626) Uncle Junior, suffering from a mental decline, watches Curb Your Enthusiasm in one episode and thinks that Larry David is supposed to be him!

(627) The original concept David Chase had for The Sopranos - when it was still a movie pitch - is that a mobster's therapist would deduce that the mobster's mother was responsible for a mafia civil war on his patch.

(628) The creators of the show Sons of Anarchy said they laced that series with Sopranos Easter eggs.

(629) David Chase makes no secret of the fact that he has loathed the television industry and television for much of his life. He even said he didn't like Northern Exposure - a show he actually produced.

(630) Steve Schirripa said he found the Tony/Dr Melfi scenes a bit boring when the show was on. He said he likes them more now.

(631) Carl Capotorto, who played Little Paulie Germani in The Sopranos, came very close to being cast as Ralph Cifaretto.

(632) Don't Stop Believin' got a lot of downloads and radio airplay when it featured in the last ever Sopranos scene. The song wasn't actually a major hit when it was first released.

(633) David Chase said he got the idea for the ducks in Tony's garden after seeing some ducks in the pool of a colleague he was working on some Rockford Files television movies with.

(634) When Danielle De Vecchio took over as Tony Soprano's sister Barbara, her first line to him included the words 'big brother' just to make audiences aware of who she was supposed to be.

(635) David Chase said they considered songs by The Kinks and Elvis Costello as the Sopranos theme before they settled on Alabama 3.

(636) Richie Aprile and Feech both cause a lot of trouble for Tony. The main reason for this is that they've both been in prison and only remember Tony as a kid. Neither of them respect his authority.

(637) Steven Van Zandt and Tony Sirico said they didn't like Salvatore 'Big Pussy' Bonpensiero being killed off because it meant they wouldn't have Vincent Pastore on the show anymore.

(638) Tony Soprano is fond of cigars and smokes a range of different ones in the show - Macanudo, Montecristos, Partagas.

(639) At the time of his death, James Gandolfini was preparing to return to television in a HBO series called Big Dead Place. Based on a book by Nicholas Johnson, the show was about workers in Antarctica.

(640) Tony Soprano ranks The Godfather Part II as the best of the trilogy. He doesn't think much of the third film.

(641) Leslie Bega played Valentina La Paz in The Sopranos. Valentina is the mistress of Ralphie and then Tony. Leslie Bega said she had wanted the part of an FBI agent in the show but ended up as Valentina - not that she was complaining because it was a bigger part.

(642) David Chase said he doesn't watch television drama shows at home. He said he tends to watch news channels.

(643) Steve Schirripa initially read for the role of FBI agent Skip Lipari.

(644) David Chase said the basic joke underpinning The Sopranos is that America has become so violent and dog-eat-dog that even a mobster has to go to therapy!

(645) Although it was mildly divisive at the time, most people seem to think now that The Sopranos ending was clever and fitting. Ending an acclaimed or popular show is not easy. Breaking Bad did it magnificently but Game of Thrones and Lost most assuredly did not.

(646) In the scene with the 'fake Livia' after the death of Nancy Marchand, Livia's dialogue doesn't really match what Tony is saying to her. It is just a few random samples of Nancy's previous dialogue in the show.

(647) Paulie is a fan of the cashmere mock-neck sweater.

(648) Tony Soprano buys his son AJ a Nissan SUV to drive.

(649) Tony Sirico always wore 'pinky rings' when he played Paulie.

(650) Tony Soprano seems very fond of Tropicana orange juice with pulp.

(651) Christopher sports some Nike tracksuits in The Sopranos.

(652) Tony Sirico as Paulie Gualtieri has 168 lines in Pine Barrens. This is the most lines in an episode that anyone, including Tony Soprano, has in season three.

(653) Patti LuPone tested for the part of Janice. Patti LuPone is an actress and singer, best known for her work on Broadway. She has won two Tony Awards for her performances in Evita and Gypsy. LuPone has also appeared in numerous films and television shows.

(654) You sometimes see Tony's crew and other 'soldiers' sitting around at construction sites in chairs doing nothing. This is known as the 'no show' job. They have fake jobs for their tax but don't actually do any work and rarely even turn up. It's like the perfect job. You get paid to do nothing!

(655) Michael Franzese, a former mobster and caporegime of the Colombo crime family in New York City, said that in real life a mob boss would never be permitted to visit a therapist like Tony Soprano does. Franzese said the real mob would fear secrets being divulged and murder both Tony Soprano and Dr Melfi!

(656) Frankie Valli was mentioned by characters in The Sopranos long before he turned up in the show playing Rusty.

(657) Grace Johnston was an early frontrunner for part of Meadow but declined the part due to school commitments. She was in the film Beaches as a child actor. These days Johnston seems to be trapped in straight to DVD style cheapie horror films.

(658) David Chase said he was more into stand alone sort of episodes than telling one long continuous story.

(659) Tony Sirico was a hypochondriac in real life. He apparently had nine doctors - all of whom he invited to the screening of the last Sopranos episode!

(660) Edie Falco joked that they should have done a spin-off show where Carmela had become the boss of the New Jersey mafia!

(661) Frank Vincent, Frankie Valli, Michael Imperioli, and Vincent Pastore were all in the 1998 television film Witness to the Mob. The film was about Sammy 'The Bull' Gravano.
Gravano is a former mobster who was associated with the Gambino crime family in New York City. He became a notorious figure in the mob world after testifying against his fellow mobsters.

(662) The Essex County executive who refused to let them shoot the episode Pine Barrens in South Mountain Reservation (because he felt The Sopranos gave Italian-Americans a bad name) was later sent to prison for corruption!

(663) An early idea David Chase had for the last ever scene was that Tony would be driving through the Lincoln Tunnel on his way to a meeting and the tunnel would suddenly go black. The darkness would signify that something bad happened to Tony at the meeting.

(664) David Chase said the Italian-American protests against The Sopranos did irritate him and make him angry.

(665) The Sopranos won 16 Emmy nominations in 1999 - winning four of them.

(666) Commendatori is an Italian term that refers to a person who has been honored with a commendation or title of respect.

(667) David Chase said the thing he knew James Gandolfini from the most before The Sopranos was the film Get Shorty.

(668) In the pilot episode we see Carmela brandish a machine gun when danger threatens. This is inconsistent with the Carmela of the series which later followed.

(669) James Gandolfini uses a different voice in the Kevin Finnerty dream sequences.

(670) Technically, Tony's mob is part of the DiMeo Crime Family. In reality, Ercole "Ecky" DiMeo has been in prison for ages and no one with that name has anything to do with Tony's mob business.

(671) Paulie describes his doctor as 'the Jonas Salk of backs. Jonas Salk was an American virologist and medical researcher who developed the first successful polio vaccine in the 1950s.

(672) We see Bobby Baccalieri's son playing the video game Max Payne. Max Payne is a third-person shooter video game series created by Finnish developer Remedy Entertainment. The first game in the series, titled Max Payne, was released in 2001 for Microsoft Windows and later ported to various other platforms.

(673) James Gandolfini's dialect coach appeared as a hospital extra in season six.

(674) Tony Soprano is a fan of Turkey Hill ice cream.

(675) Michael Imperioli said it took several episodes before he

felt safe that Christopher was going to be an ongoing part of the show and not killed off.

(676) Frank Vincent, Joe Pantoliano, and Robert Loggia all lent their voices to Grand Theft Auto 3.

(677) Tony Soprano uses the word "f***k" 155 times in season four.

(678) Michael Rispoli said he had no hard feelings when he missed out on the part of Tony Soprano because he was good friends with James Gandolfini and happy for him. He telephoned Gandolfini to congratulate him when the casting was announced.

(679) Paulie Gaultieri is promoted to Underboss in the later seasons.

(680) The mob traditionally make money through truck hijacking, robberies, loan-sharking, protection rackets etc but Tony Soprano, as a modern mob boss, also dabbles in credit card fraud and stock market scams.

(681) Before he shoots Tony, Uncle Junior says - "Cazzate, Malanga." This basically translates as "Bulls***t, Malanga."

(682) Tony's troubled mistress Gloria famous throws a London broil at Tony. London Broil is a popular dish made from a marinaded and broiled flank steak

(683) David Proval said he was so annoyed not to be cast in the first season of The Sopranos that he couldn't bring himself to watch it.

(684) Steve Schirripa said the cast on the show were always on tenderhooks about which character would be bumped off next.

(685) Michael Imperioli said he would have loved Ben Gazzara to have been in The Sopranos. Ben Gazzara was an American

actor known for his work in film, television, and stage.

(686) After the pilot, HBO took quite a long time to decide if they wanted to turn The Sopranos into a full series. The cost of producing the show was most likely the salient factor in this delay.

(687) James Lipton was considered for the part of Dr Kupgerberg (the part played by Peter Bogdanovich). James Lipton was best known as the host of the television show Inside the Actors Studio.

(688) Lorraine Bracco feared she might be annoying in the show because she was worried viewers might find the Dr Melfi scenes boring.

(689) Tony Soprano is a big animal lover in the show. This might be why Ralphie strikes a nerve when he points out that Tony is a hypocrite for posing as an animal lover when he eats meat all the time.

(690) Tony Sirico brought out his own cologne in 2008 - dubbed simply Paolo Un Uomo (Paulie For Men). It was a bit overpowering by all accounts.

(691) David Chase was apparently not happy about the marketing for The Many Saints of Newark because HBO promoted it as Young Tony Soprano film.

(692) Tony Sirico would give his co-stars a spritz of Binaca if he did a scene with them. Binaca is a brand of breath freshener.

(693) The song When It's Cold I'd Like To Die by Moby features at the end of Join the Club. This song was later used in the finale of the first season of Stranger Things when Will Byers is rescued.

(694) James Russo auditioned to play Richie Aprile. Russo has

appeared in a variety of films and television shows. He has had roles in movies like Donnie Brasco and Django Unchained.

(695) The song Con te partirò by Andrea Bocelli features prominently in Commendatori. Andrea Bocelli is an Italian opera singer, songwriter, and record producer.

(696) Jason Cerbone first appeared as Jackie Aprile Jr in season two. When the character got a larger story arc in season three they actually made Cerbone audition for the part again just to make sure he was up to the task.

(697) Annabella Sciorra was supposed to have a longer run in The Sopranos as Gloria but Sciorra missed some phone messages from David Chase asking her to come back and by the time she'd responded they'd already written her out.

(698) Ralph Cifaretto drove a dark green 1998 Lincoln Mark VIII.

(699) Frankie Valli said that appearing in The Sopranos was the highlight of his career.

(700) Edie Falco said that James Gandolfini didn't have any specific acting technique and was just a very natural actor.

(701) Lauren Bacall appeared in the Sopranos episode Luxury Lounge as herself. Lauren Bacall rose to fame in the 1940s and 1950s, appearing in films such as To Have and Have Not, The Big Sleep, and Key Largo. Bacall was known for her work with Humphrey Bogart, her husband, with whom she starred in several films.

(702) Suzanne Shepherd tested for the part of Livia. In the end she played Carmela's mother in the show.

(703) Marcia Gay Harden was considered for the part of Tony's sister Janice.

(704) Edie Falco said that acting with James Gandolfini was the most exciting experience of her career.

(705) Nancy Marchand's first acting credit was in a 1950 episode of Westinghouse Studio One. Westinghouse Studio One was a popular television anthology series that aired on CBS from 1948 to 1958.

(706) Frankie Valli said he met a few mobsters in his time and based Rusty on a real life mobster.

(707) Oksana Lada, who played Irina Peltsin, got her part in The Sopranos because her husband Slava Schoot had a role in the episode Denial, Anger, Acceptance as a Russian man and was asked if he knew any Russian speaking women who could play Tony Soprano's mistress. Slava suggested his wife Oksana!

(708) Paul Schulze, who played Father Phil Intintola, initially auditioned for the part of Mikey Palmice. Mikey is a 'soldier' in Uncle Junior's crew. Al Sapienza played Mikey in the show.

(709) Peter Riegert, who played Assemblyman Zellman, was well known for films like Animal House and Local Hero. He has had many credits over the years.

(710) David Chase said the prelude to Adriana's death is designed to slightly ambiguous at first so you don't know if Sil is really taking her to the hospital or not. However, once he leaves the main road and heads for the woods you know that Adriana is doomed.

(711) Marianne Leone tested for the part of Janice but ended up playing Joanne Moltisanti.

(712) Lorraine Bracco got second billing on The Sopranos - despite Dr Melfi not really being one of the main characters.

(713) Edie Falco said that when The Sopranos ended she got a

lot of scripts about Italian-American wives and mafia wives but turned them down because she wanted to do something different.

(714) The late music artist Prince turned down a request to use one of his songs in The Sopranos.

(715) Steve Schirripa said that James Gandolfini didn't enjoy the Tony/Livia scene with the body double standing in for the late Nancy Marchand.

(716) Edie Falco worked as a waitress when she was trying to make it as a young actor.

(717) John Ventimiglia, who played Artie Bucco, said he got offered a lot of 'Italian chef' roles after The Sopranos but turned them down because he didn't want to be typecast.

(718) Ed O'Neill was considered for the part of Richie Aprile. Ed O'Neill is best known for his roles as Al Bundy on the Fox sitcom Married... with Children and Jay Pritchett on the ABC sitcom Modern Family.

(719) The show using a double and special effects to depict Livia in a scene despite the death of Nancy Marchand may have been inspired by Ridley Scott's film Gladiator. Oliver Reed died during the production of that film so they used similar trick to complete Reed's last scenes without him.

(720) Edie Falco said she didn't hang out with The Sopranos cast much because they liked to drink and party whereas she was on the wagon and had been sober for a number of years.

(721) David Chase said that Michael Madsen was desperate to be in The Sopranos but he didn't cast him because Madsen is from Chicago and not New Jersey/New York.

(722) Michael Imperioli said that when he attended the royal premiere of the film The Lovely Bones, Prince Charles (now

obviously King Charles) told him he was a big Sopranos fan.

(723) Joe Pantoliano said that in Whoever Did This he didn't know if Ralphie had started the fire which killed Pie-O-My. The writers hadn't told him. He played the scene as if Ralphie was innocent.

(724) David Chase has confirmed that Ralphie DID start the fire which resulted in Tony killing him.

(725) Edie Falco said she was finally able to pay off her student loan when she was cast in The Sopranos.

(726) In the scene where Tony and Ralphie fight in the kitchen, James Gandolfi actually burned his hand because a stove was left on.

(727) The estate of Jimi Hendrix turned down a request to have a Hendrix song in The Sopranos.

(728) Steve Schirripa was a hotshot basketball player in his youth. He was college captain. It's difficult to picture Bobby from The Sopranos on the basketball court!

(729) The Sopranos mines comedy from many of the characters using malapropisms. A malapropism is the mistaken use of a word in place of a similar-sounding one, often with unintentionally humorous results.

(730) Michael Imperioli said that even after appearing in Goodfellas he still had to work in a restaurant to pay the bills.

(731) Edie Falco was diagnosed with breast cancer in 2003 while The Sopranos was still in production but thankfully she recovered.

(732) Michael Imperioli said that when he did his Sopranos audition he didn't really care if he got the part or not because he presumed (wrongly as it turned out) the show wouldn't last

long and probably wouldn't be much good.

(733) Jamie Lynn-Sigler assumed she would have to sing at her Sopranos audition. She had no idea that the show was about a mafia boss.

(734) David Chase said he knew right away that James Gandolfini was the best person to play Tony Soprano.

(735) The Sopranos has an audience rating of 96% on Rotten Tomatoes.

(736) GamesSpot.Com wrote of the video game The Sopranos: Road to Respect - 'The game is very linear, repetitive, and easy, which means it isn't at all fun to play. To make matters worse, the game is ugly, clunky, and full of bugs and glitches. Even if you're a devout fan of the show, there's absolutely no reason to play this game.'

(737) Before she was cast as Adriana, Drea de Matteo auditioned for the part of Tony's Russian mistress Irina Peltsin.

(738) In response to Italian-American protests against The Sopranos, Michael Imperioli said that most people were smart enough to realize these were fictional characters and only represented a minuscule fraction of the Italian-American community. The vast majority of Italian-Americans have obviously never been in the mafia!

(739) Believe it or not, you can buy a Pine Barrens custom action figure two-pack featuring Paulie and Christopher figures.

(740) Tony Sirico said that on the street everyone would call him 'Paulie' when they got an autograph or just said hello. He said he didn't mind.

(741) In what could be described as darkly ironic, Joseph

Colombo started the Italian-American Civil Rights League to protest the depiction of Italian-Americans as mobsters in film and television. In real life though Colombo was the head of the Colombo mafia family! It was all a ruse by Columbo to deflect FBI attention from himself.

(742) Robert Iler was arrested in July 2001 and charged with robbery and possession of marijuana. He pleaded guilty in April 2002 to a misdemeanor charge of petty larceny and received three years probation.

(743) James Gandolfini did his initial Tony Soprano audition above a dance studio on 79th Street. He left early though and later had to do a taped audition at the home of David Chase.

(744) David Chase said that one thing he wanted to do with the mob genre on The Sopranos that was slightly different was have bigger and more important roles for the female characters.

(745) Lorraine Bracco was famously in Goodfellas - playing Karen Hill, the wife of Ray Liotta's main character. A few years ago Lorraine attended an anniversary screening of Goodfellas and told the media that this would be the first time she had actually watched the film!

(746) Sopranos merch includes a Bada Bing! make-up bag.

(747) Tony Sirico said it never bothered him that he was typecast in mafia roles because it payed the bills!

(748) Robert Iler did home schooling when his got his part in The Sopranos. A lot of child actors seem to be home schooled.

(749) When the show ended, James Gandolfini likened himself to a sponge that had been wrung out too many times. He said that playing Tony Soprano had taken its toll.

(750) Paulie wears tracksuits in The Sopranos. This is a trait

that Tony Sirico didn't share because he said he'd never wear running gear in real life.

(751) Robert Iler is from an Irish-American family in real life but after all those years on The Sopranos he said he started picking up Italian slang and mannerisms!

(752) Tony Sirico said he had a lot of affection for the character of Paulie. He said Paulie was the sort of person you'd want next to you in the trenches because he is brave and loyal.

(753) Joe Gannascoli said he found the mustache of John Costelloe a bit bristly when they shot the Vito/Johnny Cakes scenes!

(754) Jackie Aprile Jr's death scene was probably not the finest hour of The Sopranos. He failed to notice Vito walking up behind him - despite Vito being the largest man in New Jersey!

(755) Paulie Gualtieri served in the U.S. Army Signal Corps.

(756) Edie Falco said that James Gandolofi got quite ill shooting a scene for The Sopranos one time because he ate too much ice cream as Tony!

(757) Sunday dinner is a very important meal for Tony Soprano. He insists on this family tradition being upheld.

(758) David Chase said his therapist Lorraine Kaufman helped him to understand the characters in The Sopranos - which he said made their decisions more realistic.

(759) In a 2023 article, The Hollywood Reporter ranked The Sopranos as the 2nd best show of the 21st century. Mad Men was in first place.

(760) James Gandolfini once sneaked his own wine into the Golden Globes just to make sure he had something good to drink.

(761) Edie Falco was a vegetarian (she's now a vegan) when she was in The Sopranos so she had to avoid all the meat dishes during food scenes.

(762) Billy Magnussen plays the young Paulie in The Many Saints of Newark. Billy Magnussen had a small part in the James Bond film No Time to Die.

(763) Edie Falco said she didn't really get to know James Gandolfini offscreen because he had a busy life and she was quite shy off camera. Edie thinks that because she only really knew him as Tony Soprano that actually helped her performance.

(764) Carmela's name before she married Tony was Carmela De Angelis.

(765) Michael Imperioli said that when he auditioned for The Sopranos he had no idea if it was a drama or a comedy spoof of the mafia.

(766) Tony Sirico took advantage of his Sopranos fame by appearing in numerous commercials as a Paulie Walnuts style mobster. Among the ads he did were ones for Dunkin' Donuts, Denny's, and Netflix.

(767) Local businesses and homes used for location shooting in The Sopranos all had to be compensated financially. Besides making money they were all thrilled to be in The Sopranos.

(768) The owners of the house used as Tony Soprano's house in the show built an extension while the series was in production.

(769) A big key to the success of the Sopranos is that the show was shot in New Jersey - which made it feel very authentic. A lot of famous New York set shows like NYPD Blues and Friends were actually mostly shot in Los Angeles - which is sometimes all too obvious when you watch them.

(770) David Chase said that Carmela Soprano is not a nice person because she knows full well where the money comes from for her fancy house and comfortable life. She is willing to turn a blind eye to maintain her standard of living.

(771) The opening credits of The Sopranos are clever because it seems as if Tony is driving to work but he's actually driving home. He's 'clocked off' as a mob boss but now has to 'clock on' as a father and husband.

(772) Vincent Curatola, who played Johnny Sack, said that at his Sopranos audition he could hear all the other people reading for the part of Johnny were shouting and being loud in their auditions. To be different he decided to do his audition in hushed tones. It obviously worked because he got the part.

(773) James Gandolfini was apparently considered for the part of Ben Grimm/The Thing in that forgettable 2004 Fantastic Four film. Michael Chiklis played the part in the end.

(774) Vincent Curatola said he was thirty-minutes late for his Sopranos audition but was allowed to read for the part because they thought his appearance matched the character.

(775) David Chase thinks that one of the reasons why Fox turned down The Sopranos is that they didn't think there were enough murders in it. They wanted more 'mob action'.

(776) David Chase said that one of the main reasons why the real mob declined in the United States is that longer sentences were brought in for their specific activities and they all started to 'rat' on one another to avoid languishing in prison. When the prison sentences were shorter in the old days this didn't happen so much.

(777) Steve Schirripa appeared on Celebrity Apprentice in 2009.

(778) Joe Gannascoli said he got some nice letters from gay

men about the Vito/Johnny Cakes storyline.

(779) Steve Schirripa said that when they shot the Bobby/Tony fight scene he was amazed at how strong James Gandolfini was. Steve doesn't think he would have won that fight in real life.

(780) It is very deliberate that we see Paulie getting a manicure at the start of Pine Barrens because it contrasts sharply with his bedraggled appearance later on.

(781) Federico Castelluccio, who played Furio, was an extra in the film Crocodile Dundee 2.

(782) The theme song, Woke Up This Morning by Alabama 3, was obviously written before the show came out. The lyrics are not really about gangsters but a woman in an abusive relationship.

(783) The opening credits feature the Pulaski Skyway. The Pulaski Skyway is a four-lane bridge in northern New Jersey that connects Newark and Jersey City.

(784) David Chase said that when Nancy Marchand turned up for the Livia auditions he recognized her from Lou Grant. Lou Grant was a television drama series that aired from 1977 to 1982. The show starred Ed Asner as Lou Grant, a newspaper editor who was originally a character on the comedy series The Mary Tyler Moore Show. Nancy Marchand was in 99 episodes of Lou Grant.

(785) Frank Vincent said that if a cast member had a query or wanted to change something on The Sopranos a production call would be made to David Chase - who had the final say on anything.

(786) Frank Vincent said he was a big fan of The Sopranos even before he was cast in it.

(787) David Chase has said that he doesn't think The Sopranos would get commissioned today.

(788) Tony Soprano is a big fan of the History Channel.

(789) Frank Renzulli, who was a writer and producer on The Sopranos, did some voice acting for late 1980s Real Ghostbusters cartoon.

(790) Burrata is a type of Italian cheese made from mozzarella and cream.

(791) Jessica Dunphy played AJ's girlfriend Devin Pillsbury in four episodes. Her brief role in the show might be explained by the fact that Jessica Dunphy was also in the soap opera As the World Turns at this time.

(792) GQ called The Sopranos the 'hottest' show of 2020 because it was being streamed so much during the pandemic.

(793) David Chase said that HBO wanted to cut the salary of Dominic Chianese after season one because Uncle Junior wasn't in so many scenes going forward. David said he was very annoyed when he learned of this.

(794) The contract between David Chase and HBO ended after season four. Chase said that HBO put a lot of pressure on him do a season five and in the end he decided there was still more story to tell.

(795) Anthony Cardinalle, one of the owners of the Satin Dolls nightclub which doubled for Bada Bing!, admitted to some mob connections.

(796) Some contend that the name Soprano comes from the Italian word sopra - which basically means over a hill.

(797) David Chase said that CBS was another network who wanted all the therapy stuff removed from The Sopranos

before they would consider doing it.

(798) Tony Blundetto is the maternal cousin of Tony Soprano and has just come out of prison after 16 years. Steve Buscemi memorably played this character.

(799) Capo derives from Capo regio - which means head/boss of a region.

(800) David Chase said that when he first pitched his Sopranos idea as a film his agents told him that films about the mafia were old hat.

(801) Steve Buscemi said in an interview on Charlie Rose in 2007 that he thought The Sopranos was better than most movies which get made.

(802) Kathrine Narducci auditioned for the part of Carmela. In the end she was given the part of Charmaine Bucco - Artie's wife.

(803) Jamie-Lynn Sigler said in 2022 she had started watching The Sopranos for the first time. She described it as a bittersweet experience.

(804) Some of the characters in The Sopranos are partial to a peppers and eggs sandwich. This is a popular Italian-American dish that is often enjoyed for breakfast or as a hearty and satisfying lunch option. Some variations may also include cheese, such as provolone or mozzarella.

(805) Tony Soprano shooting Tony Blundetto is what you could describe as an act of mercy. Tony B would have been tortured by Phil otherwise.

(806) Debi Mazar, who was in Goodfellas, turned down the chance to audition for the part of Carmela Soprano because she didn't want to get typecast in mafia themed roles. Debi said that in hindsight this was a mistake because The Sopranos

turned out to be much better than she expected.

(807) Steve Schirripa actually went on to be in a lot more episodes of The Secret Life of the American Teenager and Blue Bloods than he ever was on The Sopranos.

(808) Gavone means someone who is lazy or stupid - or both!

(809) Meadow jokes in The Sopranos that if things don't go well she'll end up at Glassboro State College. Glassboro State College was a public college located in Glassboro, New Jersey. In 1992, the college was renamed Rowan College of New Jersey, and in 1997 it became Rowan University. Meadow's line in the show is a bit of a goof given that Glassboro State College had changed its name several years previously.

(810) The horse that played Pie-O-My in The Sopranos was a dressage horse named Goldee. Goldee lived for many years after appearing in the show.

(811) Steve Buscemi directed four Sopranos episodes - including the classic Pine Barrens.

(812) Paulie Gualtieri was put in prison in season four because Tony Sirico was having health issues with his back and couldn't do many scenes until it was sorted out.

(813) Gabagool basically means cold cut.

(814) Steve Schirripa said that he once had to eat six steaks in a day shooting a food scene for The Sopranos!

(815) Steve Buscemi got involved in The Sopranos because David Chase was such a big fan of his 1996 film Trees Lounge. Trees Lounge featured a number of actors who went on to be in The Sopranos - Elizabeth Bracco, Michael Imperioli, John Ventimiglia, and Buscemi himself.

(816) Robert Patrick played David Scatino in The Sopranos.

David is a school friend of Tony and sporting goods store owner. He is also a compulsive gambler on a losing streak and ends up owing Tony a lot of money. Robert Patrick has been in a gazillion shows and films but is best known for playing the T-1000 liquid metal villain in Terminator 2.

(817) Goombah means comrade.

(818) It may or may not be a coincidence, but the Steve Buscemi film Trees Lounge also ends by suddenly cutting to black while a jukebox plays.

(819) David Chase said about 200 people read for the part of Livia Soprano.

(820) Steve Schirripa said that getting on The Sopranos was like 'hitting the lottery' and allowed him to be a full-time actor.

(821) Steve Buscemi said he was a bit disappointed when he learned Tony Blundetto was going to die because he had hoped to do a couple of seasons on the show.

(822) Tony's father was Giovanni "Johnny Boy" Soprano. Johnny Boy died in 1986 of emphysema. It was obviously through his father that Tony inherited his criminal empire and much of his crew.

(823) Tony's father was played by Jon Bernthal in The Many Saints of Newark. Joseph Siravo played the character in the brief flashbacks of 'Johnny Boy' in The Sopranos.

(824) Steven Van Zandt (jokingly perhaps) suggested a Bruce Springsteen song to David Chase for the last ever scene in The Sopranos. Needless to say, this didn't transpire.

(825) Gloria Trillo, who was Tony's mistress in season three, is emotionally troubled and volatile - making life difficult for Tony. This arc owes something to the thriller film Fatal Attraction.

(826) David Proval's first film role was in Martin Scorsese's Mean Streets. David Chase has said Mean Streets was an influence on The Sopranos. The film is about small-time Italian-American criminals in New York.

(827) Robert Iler said that a while after the show ended, James Gandolfini phoned Robert's agent to make sure that Robert was ok financially and career wise. Robert thought this was a nice gesture.

(828) There were three different boats used for Tony Soprano's boat in the show. The Cape Fear boat was replaced by a 43-foot Egg Harbor model in season two.

(829) James Gandolfini said he often went without sleep shooting The Sopranos because he had so much dialogue to learn.

(830) Steven Van Zandt said that the day after the last episode of The Sopranos went out he appeared on a radio show and was 'bombarded' with complaints and questions about the ending.

(831) David Chase said he didn't understand why anyone would want Tony Soprano to be killed at the end of the show because - despite all the terrible things he has done - we all sort of still like Tony.

(832) Marone basically means 'damn it'.

(833) When the last episode went out, some of the cast watched it in a giant tent in Florida as part of a Hard Rock cafe party.

(834) Robert Iler said he has never watched The Sopranos and would it too difficult to do so now after the passing of James Gandolfini.

(835) There is a great line in The Sopranos when Richie Aprile

tries to use his dead-eyed stare on Tony and Tony tells him not to give him those 'Manson lamps'. This is obviously a reference to Charles Manson. Charles Manson was an American cult leader who was responsible for a series of brutal murders orchestrated by his followers in the late 1960s. Manson formed a cult known as the Manson Family and believed in a race war that he thought would be triggered by the murders they committed.

(836) David Chase said in 2024 that he has accepted that The Sopranos is probably the best thing he will ever do. It's an impossible act to follow.

(837) Tony Soprano's boats are called The Stugots and The Stugots II. The name is Italian slang for nether regions.

(838) Edie Falco said that when she got the last ever Sopranos script and read the ending she initially thought there were pages missing! Like a lot of other people she had expected a more explosive or definitive sort of ending.

(839) David Proval, who played Richie Aprile, is not Italian-American in real life. David is of Romanian Jewish descent.

(840) Moozadell is a slang Italian word for mozzarella.

(841) When he is made the temporary boss, Silvio says that with great power comes great responsibility. This is a line that Uncle Ben has in the film Spider-Man.

(842) Aside from The Sopranos, David Proval is perhaps best known for his role as Snooze in The Shawshank Redemption.

(843) Nancy Marchand had emphysema when she was in The Sopranos. After scenes playing Livia she had to have an oxygen mask put on so she could breathe. The sight of this made Steven Van Zandt and Tony Sirico give up smoking.

(844) Robert Iler said he was at a friend's house when The

Sopranos last ever episode went out. Robert said everyone was crowding around the television to watch it but he stayed outside!

(845) The boat used as Tony Soprano's boat at the start of The Sopranos was put up for sale in 2023. The asking price was $299,900.

(846) One of the few things that Robert Iler did since The Sopranos was appear in the show Law & Order. Robert said he only took that job to get out of jury duty!

(847) Jamie-Lynn Sigler was billed as Jamie-Lynn DiScala in the season five Sopranos credits because she had got married and changed her name. She reverted back to her original name by the end of the show because the marriage didn't last very long.

(848) In the scene in Pine Barrens where Tony Soprano cracks up when Bobby appears in hunting gear, James Gandolfini was laughing for real.

(849) In the episode The Knight in White Satin Armor, Tony references Matt Helm. James Gandolfini wanted this line removed because he didn't think viewers would get the reference but David Chase kept it in. Matt Helm is a fictional secret agent who starred in thirty novels by Donald Hamilton and went to the big screen when Columbia pictures decided to jump onto the James Bond craze. In a move that probably didn't please all Helm fans, the films were spoofs with a slightly sozzled looking Dean Martin lending his laid-back style to proceedings. The Silencers (1966), Murderer's Row (1966), The Ambushers (1967), and The Wrecking Crew (1968) are sporadically entertaining but laissez faire with the source material.

(850) Steven Van Zandt said that when The Sopranos first went out his mother watched the show and had no idea that was him as Silvio Dante!

(851) Lorraine Bracco was nominated for three Golden Globes, three Emmys and three SAG Awards for her role as Dr Melfi.

(852) One of the things that makes Richie Aprile so chilling is that he is utterly fearless. In the scenes where Tony confronts him we see that Richie, despite being dwarfed by Tony Soprano, isn't the least bit intimidated or scared.

(853) James Gandolfini sold his Tony Soprano outfits at an auction in 2008 to raise money for charity. The clothes fetched $187,750.

(854) David Chase said they considered having a plot where a long lost son of (the by then late) Salvatore 'Big Pussy' Bonpensiero turns up. They didn't do this in the end though.

(855) Steven Van Zandt said that James Gandolfini found The Sopranos quite stressful because he was basically a character actor and wasn't used to having so many scenes and so much dialogue to learn.

(856) Ray Liotta said another reason he turned down a part in The Sopranos is that he didn't want to do a supporting part. If he did a television show he wanted to be the star and that obviously would have been impossible in The Sopranos because James Gandolfini was the lead actor.

(857) Will Janowitz, who played Meadow's boyfriend Finn DeTrolio, has written some screenplays with Michael Imperioli.

(858) When most of the cast were excluded from the DVD royalties, James Gandolfini gave them money from his own pocket so they didn't lose out.

(859) Michael Imperioli said he really found his groove on The Sopranos when working with Tony Sirico. The Christopher/Paulie scenes are probably the funniest in the show.

(860) Steven Van Zandt employed real life mobster John Gotti's tailor to make the suits that Silvio wears.

(861) Tony Sirico wanted to be a boxer when he was young. He fought in the Golden Gloves and in the army. He later said he was glad he gave up boxing before he got a flat nose!

(862) Michele "Feech" La Manna, played by Robert Loggia, is what is known as a Mustache Pete. Mustache Pete is a term used to refer to a member of the Italian-American mafia who was active during the early 20th century.

(863) Michael Franzese, who was a Colombo family capo in his younger years, said that the salad days of the mafia were the 1950s to the 1980s. Franzese said the mob never recovered from all the law enforcement crackdowns and is a shadow of its former self now. Tony Soprano is well aware of this new climate in The Sopranos. If he'd been a New Jersey mob boss 30 years previously he would have been a lot richer and more powerful.

(864) Joe Gannascoli described Vito Spatafore as a cross between Mike Tyson and Liberace! Joseph said that Vito was in denial about his sexuality so that's the way he approached the character's arc later on.

(865) Paulie Gualtieri often has his hands in front of him. Tony Sirico said this was something he learned in prison - always have your arms in front of you in case you need to defend yourself unexpectedly.

(866) Before he created The Sopranos, David Chase was offered the chance to adapt The Godfather novel for television. He had no interest in doing this because it had already been done brilliantly on film.

(867) Chris Rock said he turned down two approaches to appear in The Sopranos. Rock said he was enjoying the show so much as a viewer he didn't want to 'spoil' that by actually

being in it. He didn't specify which character he would have played or if he was merely being asked to play himself.

(868) Jamie-Lynn Sigler and Robert Iler, who played Tony's kids Meadow and AJ, have remained close. Jamie said she has Robert over for Christmas and Thanksgiving each year.

(869) Tony Sirico and James Gandolfini visited American troops in Iraq during the (second) Gulf War.

(870) Eddie Falco, who played Carmela, said that when she first heard about a script called The Sopranos that people were going up for she assumed the show was about singers.

(871) James Gandolfini often worked 16 hour days on The Sopranos so it got quite tiring in the end to say the least.

(872) The Sopranos depicts a world in flux, where old traditions and ways of life are shifting and decaying. Characters struggle to adapt to changing circumstances and navigate the uncertain future of the mafia world they inhabit.

(873) Lorraine Bracco wrote a book about diet and health in 2015 called To the Fullest. In the book she said she was very shaken by James Gandolfini's sudden death from a heart attack.

(874) James Gandolfini had all manner of jobs before he became famous - including a stint as a nightclub bouncer.

(875) Steven Van Zandt later starred in a Netflix show called Lilyhammer about a former gangster named Frank "The Fixer" Tagliano trying to start a new life in Norway. Steven said that James Gandolfini had agreed to make an appearance in this show but sadly his death made this impossible. Tony Sirico did appear though.

(876) Steve Schirripa wore a fat to depict the size of Bobby Baccalieri early on. Later the suit was discarded and Steve

played the role as he was (which was pretty big anyway).

(877) Jamie-Lynn Sigler was diagnosed with multiple sclerosis when she was 20 but kept it secret for a long time for fear it might harm her acting career. Multiple sclerosis (MS) is a chronic autoimmune disease that affects the central nervous system, specifically the brain and spinal cord. Symptoms of multiple sclerosis can vary widely and may include fatigue, numbness or tingling, muscle weakness, difficulty walking, coordination and balance problems, vision problems, cognitive changes, and pain.

(878) Dominic Chianese, who played Uncle Junior in The Sopranos, was in The Godfather Part II. He played Johnny Ola. Johnny Ola is an associate of Hyman Roth and plays a key role in the plot of the film.

(879) Tony Sirico was also in The Godfather Part II as an extra.

(880) David Chase only directed two episodes of The Sopranos.

(881) Made In New Jersey was considered as the title of the show.

(882) The original intention of David Chase was to have Tony suffocate his mother Livia in the show. He changed this plan though because Nancy Marchand, who had been diagnosed with cancer, requested that she be kept in the show because she liked being a part of it and loved acting. As a consequence of this Livia remained in the show until Nancy Marchand passed away in real life.

(883) Drea de Matteo said she had to rush away from a family Sunday dinner to do her last Sopranos audition. She was called in unexpectedly.

(884) When it comes to music, David Chase said that Tony

Soprano is a 'classic rock' sort of person.

(885) The Pine Barrens has been designated as a National Reserve to protect its ecological and historical significance.

(886) David Chase said he chose Journey's song Don't Stop Believin' for the final scene in The Sopranos because the crew hated the song!

(887) Another actor was initially cast as Ralphie Cifaretto because a fee couldn't be agreed with first choice Joe Pantoliano. However when a deal was agreed the other actor was let go and Pantoliano reshot the four episodes of scenes that had been shot with the other actor.

(888) The actor was was cast as Ralphie Cifaretto but then let go was Robert Funaro. Robert was though given the part of Eugene Pontecorvo in the show.

(889) The humble DVD player is seen as a sign of status (albiet modest status) in The Sopranos. This is because DVDs were fairly new at the time.

(890) If you take out the fact he's a mob boss (which is obviously something 99.9% of people can't relate to), Tony Soprano is quite relatable because he has many of the same problems as us. Marriage, kids, his relationship with his mother, money, anxiety, adjusting to a changing world, trying to find some sense of meaning in life. And so on.

(891) Paulie Gualtieri considers himself to be more sophisticated than your average person due to being of Italian descent. However, when Paulie visits the real Italy we see that the Italians see him as little more than some uncultured American oaf.

(892) Tony Soprano's love of old gangster films comes from David Chase's love of them too.

(893) David Chase said he encountered some mafia 'wiseguys' in his younger years and was always intrigued by these men and their strange lifestyle.

(894) Michael Gandolfini said he had never watched The Sopranos until he was cast in The Many Saints of Newark. In preparation for playing the young Tony he DID watch the show. Michael said watching The Sopranos was a strange and poignant experience because he was obviously watching his late father in the show.

(896) The mafia began as a secret society to protect the interests of local landowners.

(897) Steve Schirripa said he put off buying an apartment in New York when he joined The Sopranos because he genuinely had no idea if his character was going to get killed off quickly or stick around.

(898) You can buy a number of Sopranos themed jigsaw puzzles.

(899) The mafia operates on a strict code of conduct known as Omertà, which emphasizes loyalty, secrecy, and silence.

(900) Jamie-Lynn Sigler was asked to put on weight during The Sopranos because they felt that Meadow was way too thin for a girl who grew up in an Italian home where food is important. Jamie-Lynn Sigler said this request helped her to accept she had an eating disorder.

(901) Steve Schirripa was in the last ever Columbo with Peter Falk. This was 2003's Columbo Likes the Night Life. Steve played, yes, you guessed it, a mobster.

(902) The racing video game AJ is playing in the episode Bust Out is Flag To Flag.

(903) It has been alleged that the reason why Marcia Gay

Harden wasn't cast as Janice Soprano is that she was considered too 'sexy' to be Tony's sister.

(904) In an interview during the pandemic lockdowns, the English pop star Charli XCX said she was watching three episodes of The Sopranos a day.

(905) Tony Blundetto says in the show that he was called Ichabod Crane by other kids when he was younger. Ichabod Crane is a fictional character and protagonist in Washington Irving's short story "The Legend of Sleepy Hollow." He is a superstitious and awkward schoolteacher who falls in love with Katrina Van Tassel, but also finds himself in a rivalry with a menacing ghost known as the Headless Horseman. Ichabod Crane is known for his thin and tall appearance.

(906) As part of the 25th anniversary of The Sopranos in 2024, there was a pop up Satriale's in New York and Los Angeles.

(907) Lillo Brancato, who was discovered by Robert De Niro for his film A Bronx Tale, played Matthew Bevilaqua in The Sopranos. Bevilaqua worked under Christopher. Lillo Brancato is known for his legal troubles following a 2005 incident in which he was involved in a burglary that resulted in the death of an off-duty police officer. Brancato was convicted of attempted burglary and sentenced to ten years in prison, but was released on parole in 2013. His acting career has never recovered.

(908) The character Hesh was loosely based on Morris Levy. Morris Levy was a music executive and the owner of the infamous independent record label Roulette Records. He was known for his involvement in various illegal activities, including mob connections and music piracy. Levy was also a controversial figure in the music industry, with many artists accusing him of unfair business practices and withholding their royalties. He passed away in 1990 at the age of 62.

(909) Frank Vincent and Joe Pesci were actually a stage

comedy double-act in the early 1970s called Vincent and Pesci. After watching Casino, I'd be pretty terrified if these two came out on stage together!

(910) Some academic theories have drawn parallels between Tony Soprano and Gatsby - from F Scott Fitzgerald's The Great Gatsby. The Great Gatsby was published in 1925. The story is set during the early part of the Roaring Twenties, the Jazz Age. A time of great prosperity for America. Wild parties, prohibition, bootleggers, new money, people becoming rich. It isn't destined to last though. The great stock market crash of 1929 is just around the corner and will serve as the sober hangover and symbolic ending for this glitter strewn decade of excess. The shadows are already beginning to loom well before in the story. It's an era that can't possibly last forever. So the novel is a snapshot of the age amongst a particular money washed strata of American society before it all goes belly up. They don't realise that happiness doesn't come with having money in the bank, a famous family or reside at the bottom of a champagne bottle.

Sometimes it's much more complicated than that. The less fashionable West Egg is where those with new money live and Nick finds his modest house situated next to the grand mansion of the mysterious and enigmatic Gatsby. Gatsby throws huge swanky champagne sozzled parties at his mansion for the fashionable and rich but he's never actually seen at any of them enjoying himself or taking part in the revelry. One of the principle themes in the novel is the emptiness of the American Dream. The pursuit of wealth and popularity. Money does not buy you peace of mind or make you happy. You can be the richest person in the world but wealth can't always buy you the things you want - or think you want.

(911) James Gandolfini was only five years older than Michael Imperioli in real life. Christopher seems much younger than Tony in the show.

(912) The Pine Barrens in New Jersey is associated with the legend of the Jersey Devil. The Jersey Devil is a creature said to reside in the Pine Barrens. Legend has it the monster is the unwanted 13th son of an early settler who made a pact with the Devil. The Jersey Devil is described as having hooves, scaly wings and a goat like head. There have been several alleged sightings and reports of the creature - most famously in 1909 when strange hooved footprints in the snow abounded and created some panic (though this incident is believed to have been hoaxed). The Jersey Devil is part of local folklore and legend and has inspired films like The Last Broadcast. Attempts to prove the existence of the fanciful creature (a large reward was once offered for some of its dung!) have yet to yield any notable results.

Joseph Bonaparte, the brother of Napoleon, was exiled to the United States and settled in New Jersey. While out hunting one day in the woods he is said to have encountered a winged creature with hooves and a horse like head. Joseph took a shot at the creature with his rifle and it flew off. When he described this encounter to locals they told hinm that he had come face to face with the Jersey Devil. The Jersey Devil is an enjoyable piece of New Jersey folklore but one to be taken with a pinch of salt. There are certainly no convincing photographs or film footage of the creature in existence but if you ever find yourself in the Pine Barrens you'd best stay alert - just in case the creature is lurking somewhere.

(913) Little Carmine Lupertazzi mentions Ben Kingsley's performance in Sexy Beast in the episode Luxury Lounge. Sexy Beast is a cult 2000 British crime film directed by Jonathan Glazer. The film follows a retired criminal, played by Ray Winstone, whose peaceful life in Spain is disrupted when a violent, terrifying and unpredictable former associate, played by Ben Kingsley, arrives and demands his involvement in a heist.

(914) A popular fan theory is that Patsy had Tony 'whacked' at the end of The Sopranos. Tony had Patsy's twin brother

whacked - lest we forget.

(915) After the show ended, James Gandolfini said he found the violence in the show quite difficult and wouldn't like to play another mafia character.

(916) Janice Soprano was in an ashram in Los Angeles. An Ashram is a spiritual hermitage or a religious retreat for those seeking spiritual growth and enlightenment.

(917) The Many Saints of Newark was simultaneously released in theaters and on HBO Max. Most people chose the streaming option and the cinema release drew very modest totals.

(918) Joe Pantoliano was only available to play Ralphie Cifaretto in The Sopranos because the Wachowskis decided not to bring him back for The Matrix sequels.

(919) The booth used by Tony Soprano and his family in the last ever scene in The Sopranos sold for $82,000 at an auction in 2024.

(920) In a 2024 interview, David Chase said that (in his view) television was getting 'dumb' again and the streaming giants were producing a large amount of mediocre content.

(921) When the Game of Thrones television adaptation was pitched to HBO it was described as 'The Sopranos in Tolkien's Middle-Earth'.

(922) In September 2000, a coalition of Italian-American groups protested outside HBO's headquarters. They argued that The Sopranos compounded the worst stereotypes of the Italian American community and should be taken off the air.

(923) David Chase said he hasn't closed the door on the possibility of doing another prequel featuring Tony in his younger years.

(924) Bobby "Baccala" Baccalieri Jr has the most appearances in the show out of all the characters who didn't appear in season one.

(925) Michael Imperioli was another cast member who said Uncle Junior was his favorite character.

(926) The film that Uncle Junior is watching in Members Only is Paths of Glory. Paths of Glory is a 1957 film directed by Stanley Kubrick, based on the novel of the same name by Humphrey Cobb. The film follows a group of French soldiers during World War I who are put on trial for cowardice after a failed mission to capture a German stronghold. The film stars Kirk Douglas.

(927) Steve Schirripa said the set catering on The Sopranos was amazing and it was mostly (as you might expect) Italian food.

(928) Paulie Gualtieri refers to Vito as "Bluto" in Mayhem. Bluto is the character played by John Belushi in the John Landis comedy film Animal House.

(929) Those who talk about the decline of the mob often cite RICO as a salient factor. The Racketeer Influenced and Corrupt Organizations (RICO) Act is a federal law that was enacted in 1970 to combat organized crime, including mafia operations.

(930) James Gandolfini would apparently do some method acting by staying up all night to look authetically tired when there where scenes where Tony did the same thing.

(931) Down Neck is the only Sopranos episode directed by a woman. This episode was directed by Lorraine Senna.

(932) The team who made The Sopranos had to learn about money laundering before they wrote the show because this is a big part of Tony Soprano's business arrangements. Money

laundering is the process of concealing the origins of illegally obtained money, typically by transferring it through a complex series of banking transactions or commercial activities. This illegal activity is often used by criminals to legitimize their ill-gotten gains and make them appear as though they were obtained through legal means.

(933) David Chase said that when he was still thinking of The Sopranos as film (which had its focus on a mobster who has therapy) he pictured Robert De Niro and Anne Bancroft in the lead parts.

(934) Will Janowitz, who played Meadow's boyfriend Finn DeTrolio, has worked a lot since the show. He was in Boardwalk Empire and also did voice acting on some of the GTA games.

(935) The expression/name "bada bing" in The Sopranos comes from James Caan's character in The Godfather. This term predates The Godfather though and may derive from the Italian word bada bene - which loosely translates as good morning. The term is used as an exclamation - drumsticks on a drum. Bada bing!

(936) A mafia 'sit-down' is a meeting between leaders or members of a mafia organization to discuss and make decisions on important matters related to their criminal activities. This could include issues such as territorial disputes, resolving conflicts, sharing profits, or planning criminal activities. The sit-down is often held in a private and secure location to ensure the safety and confidentiality of the participants. It is a key ritual within the mafia culture and is essential for maintaining order and hierarchy within the organization.

(937) Georgianne Walken, who did the casting on The Sopranos, is the wife of the actor Christopher Walken.

(938) HBO, or Home Box Office, is a premium cable and

streaming service known for producing and broadcasting original television shows and films. HBO was launched on November 8, 1972, as a pay television service that aired movies and sporting events. In its early years, HBO faced challenges from regulators and competitors, but it successfully grew its subscriber base and expanded its programming offerings. Throughout the 1980s and 1990s, HBO gained a reputation for producing high-quality original programming, such as The Sopranos, Sex and the City, and Six Feet Under. These shows helped establish HBO as a leader in the television industry and paved the way for other cable networks to create their own original content.

(939) In the episode The Strong, Silent Type, Christopher tells Tony that with his diet he'll be dead of a heart attack at 50. James Gandolfini was 51 when he died of a heart attack in real life.

(940) The correct way to say Steve Buscemi's surname is boo-SHEM-ee.

(941) James Gandolfini's pay dispute with HBO before season five got so knotty that at one point Gandolfini claimed he wasn't even under contract to do season five and could walk away if he chose to. Gandolfini and his representatives did have grounds to ask for a pay hike because some stars of other popular television shows at the time - like Ray Romano (in Everyone Loves Raymond) and Kelsey Grammer (in Frasier) - were being paid double and treble what James was getting as Tony Soprano.

(942) Vincent Pastore, who played Salvatore Bonpensiero, launched his own pasta sauce in 2020. The sauce used Italian tomatoes and contained no sugar.

(943) Tony Blundetto and Phil Leotardo make their first appearances in The Two Tonys.

(944) David Chase said the first season of The Sopranos was

basically the plot of the film idea he had about a mobster who seeks therapy because his mother is driving him mad.

(945) Joe Gannascoli, who played Vito Spatafore, hosts private dinners for fans. If you hire him he'll cook you pasta (he's a trained chef) and regale you with Sopranos trivia.

(946) The whole of the Sopranos runs to roughly 86 hours.

(947) Tony Sirico and Steven Van Zandt were the last two cast members to sign up for the last eight episodes because they had a salary dispute with HBO. Given that the show was coming to an end you couldn't really blame them for wanting as good a last deal as possible.

(948) We see Tony Soprano get teary eyed in one episode watching Band of Brothers - which was a big HBO miniseries in 2001. Band of Brothers tells the true story of Easy Company, a unit of the 506th Parachute Infantry Regiment in the 101st Airborne Division during World War II. The series follows the soldiers from their training in Georgia to their harrowing experiences fighting the Germans on the Western European battlefront .

(949) Tony Soprano's original name Tommy Soprano was going to be a homage to Tom Powers - James Cagney's character in The Public Enemy.

(950) In the therapy scenes with Tony and Dr Melfi, David Chase asked for the camera to be very still so that these scenes contrasted with the rest of the show.

(951) Holsten's diner in Bloomfield, where the last ever Sopranos scene was shot, didn't actually have onion rings on their menu in real life. They did add them afterwards though.

(952) During the run of The Sopranos, David Chase signed a deal that gave him a cut of the profits from Sopranos DVD sales. This was a shrewd move because that must have netted a

fair penny in those pre-streaming days.

(953) Aida Turturro, who played Tony's sister Janice, knew James Gandolfini long before The Sopranos because they were in A Streetcar Named Desire on the stage together.

(954) A Vulture article in 2019 ranked the season three episode University as the best ever Sopranos episode.

(955) Michael Imperioli provides a 'beyond the grave' narration to The Many Saints of Newark as Christopher Moltisanti.

(956) Aida Turturro, who played Tony's sister Janice, said she improvised some lines during her Sopranos audition and was told she wouldn't be hired if she didn't stick to the script.

(957) You can buy FUNKO POPS of characters from The Sopranos.

(958) You can buy Sopranos Monopoly. The blurb is - 'Call the shots in MONOPOLY: The Sopranos, based on the Emmy award-winning mob drama! Buy, sell, and trade popular locations like Tony Soprano's House and Satriale's Pork Store, before wheeling and dealing at The Bada Bing! Let tokens like The Stugots or Bobby Bacala's toy train engine take you around the board and be the last boss standing!'

(959) After the end of The Sopranos, Jamie-Lynn Sigler played herself in 13 episodes of Entourage.

(960) The only episode that Carmela wasn't in is Where's Johnny?

(961) Newark in New Jersey is about 20 miles from New York City.

(962) David Chase chose Woke Up This Morning by Alabama 3 as the show's theme song after he heard on a Los Angeles

radio station.

(963) Jamie-Lynn Sigler was worried she might be replaced on The Sopranos because of her eating disorder. It turned out though that everyone was very supportive and helped her get better.

(964) Mad-don is an Italian expression to express surprise. A reference to Madonna - not the singer!

(965) The production of the last batch of episodes of The Sopranos was delayed by two months because James Gandolfini had knee surgery.

(966) Vincent Pastore, who played Salvatore 'Big Pussy' Bonpensiero, said that David Chase was planning to make a Sopranos movie around 2013 but it never happened because James Gandolfini unexpectedly passed away.

(967) Bobby Baccalieri makes his first appearance in the season two episode Do Not Resuscitate.

(968) Tony Soprano's Cadillac Escalade from the show was put up for sale in 2022. The asking price was $175,000.

(969) The Sopranos video game Road to Respect features Big Pussy's son, Joey LaRocca.

(970) Christa Helm was a bit part actress whose roles included a small part in the TV show Wonder Woman. She was also in the 1974 horror film Legacy of Satan. Christa apparently kept a diary which detailed all of her private encounters with the rich and famous. She considered this diary to be like a sort of pension or life insurance. It would make a juicy memoir or lucrative newspaper article one day. On the night of February the 12th, 1977, Christa went to a Hollywood party in Laurel Canyon with her roommate Stephanie. At some point, Christa left the party. She was later found stabbed to death outside of her agent Sandy Smith's house. She was 27 years-old (there's

that old curse again - a LOT of famous people, if one could call Christa famous, have died at the age of 27). Christa was stabbed 23 times and also beaten with a heavy object. Sandy Smith was allegedly asleep and heard nothing. Christa's blood splattered body was found by a young man who walked through that street shortly after the murder. Believe it or not, one of the people interviewed by the police in relation to Christa's murder was Tony Sirico. Tony Sirico (who obviously turned out to be innocent) was one of the last people to visit Christa before her death. The murder remains unsolved but those who knew Christa thought the prime suspect was her old flame Patsy Collins - who was a backup singer and lover to Christa. The police never spoke to Patsy Collins about this murder because they had had no idea where she was. Modern forensic testing on this case has suggested that Christa had female DNA under her nails when she died. This would obviously tally with the Patsy Collins theory.

(971) Christian Maelen was the voice of Joey LaRocca in The Sopranos video game. Maelen was actually in the running to play Christopher Moltisanti in the television show.

(972) The Sopranos is a bit like The Walking Dead in that it took inspiration from a film (Scorsese's Goodfellas) and turned it into a long form television show - much in the way The Walking Dead took inspiration from George Romero's zombie movies and did the same. Interestingly, Scorsese said he didn't like The Sopranos and couldn't get into it and Romero was also equally indifferent to The Walking Dead, having nothing nice to say about that show.

(973) Martin Scorsese said he couldn't get into The Sopranos because he couldn't relate to it. He said that having modern day mobsters living in big houses in New Jersey didn't feel like the real mafia to him - or at least the mafia he was familiar with.

(974) David Chase said he wasn't sure if Tony's rather plush house in the Sopranos was realistic for a mob boss. Some real

life mob bosses lived in very modest houses because they didn't want to draw any attention to themselves.

(975) The Satin dolls strip club, which doubled for Bada Bing!, sold some of the poles used in The Sopranos when the show ended.

(976) The New York Times, in their review of the last ever episode, called the ending a 'prank' by David Chase. David Chase denied that the ending was designed to baffle or irritate people. He didn't understand what all the fuss was about.

(977) Steve Schirripa lived in Las Vegas when he was first cast in the show. He actually had to pay his own travel expenses - which turned out to be higher than his fee (meaning he was essentially working for nothing at first). In the end though they arranged for Steve to be accomodated closer to the set during shooting so that he wouldn't have to lose out on money.

(978) Steven Van Zandt went back on tour with the E Street Band when The Sopranos was still in production. Steven said that this meant Silvio Dante was in less scenes than planned. David Chase arranged for Steven to shoot his Sopranos scenes during his breaks from the tour.

(979) Season four is the first season where Dr Melfi is not in the top ten when it comes to characters with the most lines.

(980) Silvio Dante ranks seventh overall when it comes to characters with the most lines.

(981) David Chase was very angry when he learned that The Many Saints of Newark was going to be streamed on HBO Max at the same time as the cinema release. David said it was designed as a film for cinemas and he was saddened that fewer people would now experience it that way.

(982) When he goes into hiding, Vito Spatafore calls himself 'Vince' and tries to start a new life in New Hampshire. He even

gets a normal job. However, Vito soon begins to find life as a 'civilian' absolutely tedious and yearns to go back to being a capo in the mob. This plot thread shows us how seductive the mob is to people like Vito. He loves the money, excitement, and hustle bustle of mob life. He loves the late nights and card games. It is almost impossible for someone like Vito to just be an Average Joe living a quiet mundane life in some out of the way place. Of course, this all comes back to bite Vito because the downside of life in the mob is the danger. Trying to get back into the mob turns out to be a huge mistake.

(983) In the classic scene where Meadow's boyfriend Finn tells Tony's crew about Vito being gay, Tony gives Finn some money and tells him to go and get a soda and any sandwich he likes. What makes this moment funny is that Will Janowitz (who played Finn) was in his early twenties and yet Tony is acting as if this is a ten year-old kid!

(984) The Sopranos was seen by some critics to have parallels with King Lear. King Lear is a tragedy play written by William Shakespeare. It tells the story of an aging king who decides to divide his kingdom among his three daughters, based on how much they profess their love for him. The play explores themes of power, family relationships, madness, and betrayal.

(985) The 1999 mafia themed comedy Mickey Blue Eyes with Hugh Grant featured a number of actors who would also be in the Sopranos. Burt Young, Tony Sirico, John Ventimiglia, Aida Turturro, Joe Gannascoli, Vincent Pastore.

(986) We see Christopher watching Three Amigos! in The Sopranos when he's a bit doolally after snorting some heroin. Three Amigos! is a 1986 Western comedy film directed by John Landis and starring Steve Martin, Chevy Chase, and Martin Short. The film follows three silent film actors who are mistaken for real-life heroes by a small Mexican village and must defend the village from a notorious bandit.

(987) Michele DeCesare, who played Meadow's friend Hunter

in six episodes, is the daughter of David Chase.

(988) James Gandolfini managed a few nightclubs before he became an actor.

(989) The song Woke Up this Morning was written by Alabama 3 about a real life crime case that took place in 1996. Sara Thornton was convicted of murdering her abusive husband, Malcolm Thornton, by stabbing him to death in their home in England. During the trial, Sara claimed that she had killed her husband in self-defense after suffering years of physical and emotional abuse at his hands. However, the jury found her guilty of murder and she was sentenced to life in prison. The case sparked a national debate about domestic violence and the justice system's handling of cases involving abused women who turn to violence to protect themselves. Many supporters argued that Sara had been failed by the system and should have been treated as a victim rather than a criminal. After serving six years of her life sentence, Sara was released on parole in 2003.

(990) The point of the ending to The Sopranos, with the screen cutting to black, is that we don't know if the man Tony Soprano was looking at was about to shoot him or merely another patron in the eatery. And that's what life is like being Tony Soprano.

(991) Drea de Matteo said that Steven Van Zandt was very uncomfortable shooting the scene where Sil drags Adriana out of the car to shoot her. He was worried he might hurt her by accident.

(992) During the pandemic, HBO reported that viewership of The Sopranos had gone up by 179% on their streaming service.

(993) Richie Aprile makes his first appearance in the season two episode Toodle-F***ing-Oo.

(994) Michael Imperioli said he doesn't like watching violence

and blood in films or television shows. Violence was obviously necessary in The Sopranos though because we have to see the harsh realities of mob life.

(995) Tony Sirico's one condition for playing Paulie is that Paulie would never became a rat (informant) in the show.

(996) David Chase wanted the Sopranos opening titles to have a different song each week. This obviously never happened in the end but the closing credits do have a range of different songs.

(997) Christopher Moltisanti's last car in the show is a Cadillac Escalade EXT.

(998) The Writers Guild of America voted The Sopranos the best written television show of all time in 2013.

(999) David Chase and the writers on the show said there were only three logical ways to conclude The Sopranos. Tony either dies, goes to prison, or just carries on as normal. In the end they went for a slightly ambiguous ending where all of these things are still possible for Tony.

(1000) It's fair to say that no one could have played Tony Soprano as perfectly and brilliantly as James Gandolfini did.